THE PERFECT MANGO

Before you start to read this book, take this moment to think about making a donation to punctum books, an independent non-profit press

@ https://punctumbooks.com/support

If you're reading the e-book, you can click on the image below to go directly to our donations site. Any amount, no matter the size, is appreciated and will help us to keep our ship of fools afloat. Contributions from dedicated readers will also help us to keep our commons open and to cultivate new work that can't find a welcoming port elsewhere. Our adventure is not possible without your support.

Vive la Open Access.

Fig. 1. Hieronymus Bosch, *Ship of Fools* (1490–1500)

First published in 2019 by 3Ecologies Books/Immediations, an imprint of punctum books.
https://punctumbooks.com

ISBN-13: 978-1-950192-13-7 (print)
ISBN-13: 978-1-950192-14-4 (ePDF)

LCCN: 2019932679
Library of Congress Cataloging Data is available from the Library of Congress

Book design: Vincent W.J. van Gerven Oei
Cover image: Erin Manning, *Rape* (1994)

HIC SVNT MONSTRA

Erin
Manning

The Perfect
Mango

Contents

Preface

I wrote *The Perfect Mango* over nineteen days in July 1994. Living had always been hard, but I had hit an impasse. The lure of ending it all was very strong. Suicide was always close, had always lived on the edges. Today it is more a lurker than a temptation. Then it felt more like a command, and while much of the time I could resist attempting it, there had been more than one occasion where I couldn't. The nineteen days through which I wrote my body, the days of bringing *The Perfect Mango* into the world, were days I gave myself fully to the possibility of life.

The words written here, breathless, are not the words I would compose today. I hesitated deeply before republishing the book, afraid that the words would haunt me, afraid of their unrelenting rawness. I wanted to sculpt them, to orient them, to write in pauses where a distance could be crafted that might mute the messy scream I hear when I return to them. But these are not words that can be edited. These are words that gave me nineteen days, that gave me life. They are words that bear witness to the struggle of finding a way to speak of the moreness that is a body, the fissure where pain and desire meet. For the body that says I throughout this work is never a single body, never a body that stands alone, that knows itself as an individual, and this is, I think, what can be heard in the unrelenting sentences, in the breathlessness of a composition that asks how else life might be lived.

To allow words like these to find their way back into the world is to want to give voice to those moments of messy survival that call for a proposition such as this one. These were the conditions: to write one chapter a day, fully edited, and write until the living became possible. When I read these words, these imperfect, grasping, gasping calls for new modes of existence, this is what I hear. I hear a call for other ways of listening to the urgency that is living.

It took me almost twenty-five years to return to *The Perfect Mango*. Relieved by its disappearance, I preferred to have it in the shadows and to craft the life I have lived since with more distance from the pain and the terrible brokenness that comes with sexual assault and all that follows from it. It was Brian who said the book was ready to reappear. And it was Julietta who gave me the courage to read it again. What I have learned from this encounter with those who hear the words I wrote so long ago is that it may not be my decision to make whether this imperfect and deeply honest book finds its place in the world once again. For *The Perfect Mango* is in no real sense mine: it is the force that gave me life, the springboard through which I could begin to speak.

Emergent seas

The speaking has not been easy, but I've noticed that over the past few years it has come more fluidly, the stories intertwined with the concepts crafted over years of asking how else living is possible.

In February 2019 I will turn fifty. This turn will mark twenty-five years since I wrote *The Perfect Mango*. In 1994 and for many years afterwards every year that was marked by a birthday felt like a surprise. I didn't think I would know the world from this vantage point. But I have moved in the spiral of time, have lived another cycle and here, close to fifty, I am moved by what age can do. Many of us are taught that age reduces us, that it depletes us.

This is not my experience. Growing older has come with a sense that the multiplicity of I which was so difficult for me as a child is truly the richness life brings. There is no single identity, only a policing of the category. This is what changes: we may become less willing to fit into the categories imposed on our bodies.

With that comes the joy of not being a victim. Joy here is meant in the Spinozist sense. Joy is not happiness. It is the capacity of the world to bring with it what exceeds the actual. It is the more-than of experience in the making. I think I always knew this joy, and it was this unwieldy moreness that I was trying to touch in *The Perfect Mango.* I had no words for it then, though Nietzsche certainly was a muse, as he remains for me today.

I say "not being a victim" not to deny that terrible things happened or that I suffered. I mean that to be a victim is to stand still, to hold oneself to a frame, a category. What *The Perfect Mango* gave me was a way to move, a way to find a rhythm that could pull me into new directions.

These directions did not come easily. There were many years after *The Perfect Mango* that were difficult, and the threat of suicide never completely leaves me, even now. But much has changed, and this change has come through years of practice. I think of practice here as a mode of experimentation that produces orientations life can unfold. Practice includes art and writing, it includes working with materials and crafting concepts. But it also includes the work of the quotidian. I learned to compose with others for whom the collective is more-than the sum of its parts. I learned to seed collaborations that welcomed a more-than-I, collaborations that could give life without reducing life to a single living being. I needed this: to be in excess of myself.

To be in excess of myself is to be embroiled in a process that makes me. It is to feel the world moving me, shifting the contours of what me might be. There is no victimhood here. Certainly there is inheritance and with it there are directions best not followed. I am careful to collaborate with the forces of existence and not the categories, not the frames that would return me to a cage I have worked so hard to leave behind.

At almost-fifty I no longer struggle as much with self-destructiveness because I am not as close as I was to a notion of self. Much of the time I is elsewhere, captured by the lure of an orientation too rich to pass by. This is also what comes with age, I think – the precision of orientation. Today I follow the lead that takes me where the world worlds.

When Brian and I met, he saw me like no one had ever seen me. Shortly after we got together, he gave me a book: *When Rabbit Howls* by Truddi Chase and her alters. It's been many years since I read the book, but what struck me most was the force of rabbit. Rabbit is the unspeakable force that cleaves a body open, that keeps it alive. It is that wild interloper that accompanies those who have been broken and haunts them, the force that unrelentingly expresses that which cannot be spoken.

Re-reading *The Perfect Mango* I could hear rabbit. Rabbit is less present now. Sometimes I feel the force of rabbit still, especially on the nights when the nightmares return or in conditions of violence when the body closes down and moves like a terrorized animal in flight. I don't mind rabbit so much anymore. I recognize that it is rabbit that kept me alive. It is rabbit that saw what so few others were prepared to see.

Sexual abuse and abuse of all kinds breaks the body. It cleaves experience into a before and after. In my case, though, time was much more crooked. What is an experience that takes you with it? How to speak of acts that multiply, of ways of living that seem to call them forth? How to speak of a life poised for the unraveling?

In the intervening years I have found few answers to those questions. It turns out these are not the questions that most trouble me today. What I want to know today is how to create conditions for living beyond humanism's fierce belief that we, the privileged, the neurotypicals, the as-yet-unscathed, the able-bodied, hold the key to all perspectives in the theatre of living. The conditions for living I seek are those that facilitate a more-than-human encounter with a life lived in the kind of creative activity that deeply challenges the normative standards that enable the violence I experienced as a child and continued to experience throughout my adolescence and early adulthood. This violence is lived everyday not only by those who are abused, but by all for whom the world as we know it remains out of reach – those whose subjectivities are excluded from the category of the human. I don't want to participate in that world. I want to live at the interstices where black life and indigenous life and neurodiverse life and all ways of living that invent ways of encountering the force of what living can be are celebrated. I want to live in the fierce celebration of a world invented by those modes of life which tear at the colonial, white, neurotypical fabric of life as we know it.

In the mix, no category will remain untouched. Categories imprison bodies. The me-ness of the intervening twenty-five years has sidled many identities, many forms. But what is clear to me now is that the freedom of aging is the recognition that these forms are much more temporary than we might have thought, and the staging of those forms much more brittle than we might have imagined. There is a world to be invented, a world always being invented, and this is the world that keeps me alive today.

.

Whoever writes in blood and aphorisms does not want to be read but to be learned by heart. In the mountains the shortest way is from peak to peak: but for that one must have long legs. Aphorisms should be peaks – and those who are addressed, tall and lofty. The air is thin and pure, danger near, and the spirit full of gay sarcasm: these go well together. I want to have goblins around me, for I am courageous. Courage that puts ghosts to flight creates goblins for itself: courage wants to laugh.

— Friedrich Nietzsche, *Thus Spoke Zarathustra*

The Body

These words are written on my body. They are twenty-five-year-old words and sometimes they have lived a thousand years. I have been waiting to write this book, waiting all my life for it to stop long enough so that I can transpose these words aching, marking, devouring me. Today I write my body.

I know I have written this before, that it has been written before me and in the thousand years and twenty-five I will write it many more times. Today I write my story, written among the maze of paint and vomit that is my life today, a story of love and desire and fear and weakness.

Often I wonder whether my teeth are rotting. Is that the mark of my story on my body? My story ravages my body every time I try to read it, exposing the traces of time left behind, the unfinished fantasies and dreams come true.

On Tuesday I had my hair cut. I had curls. I cut them off. I wanted my face exposed, open to the world. No more curls and perhaps they will never come back. They liked my curls, as they like the painting of the street in Barcelona. It soothes them and they feel understood. When they don't understand they turn away. When I don't understand, I throw up.

I'm throwing up today. It seems strange to be throwing up the day I finally begin to write the book that has been waiting for so long, but I am. It's a slow process. It takes almost as long as eating. Perhaps it's rotting my teeth.

Once I wrote another book. It was about a sea that disappeared, about a boy who believed in a beautiful purple sea, about parents who didn't see, about a sea that disappeared. There were pictures as well, painted in watercolour. I don't have the book anymore. It was stolen. Perhaps it is the mark on my left thigh, the one that looks like cellulite. It's not cellulite at all. It's my lost story, waiting to be read again. But I can't read it because every time I open a magazine I read about the new magical cure to eliminate cellulite. They don't want to read my book. They want to unwrite the writing on my body and make me whole again. They want to polish me up and make me smooth, nice to look at, appealing and unthreatening. In my book the sea disappeared because they couldn't see. Perhaps my book was smeared by their creams and not stolen at all. Perhaps they will make this one invisible with their magic wrinkle creams. This book is full of wrinkles.

Throwing up isn't easy today. There is too much to throw up and my body is tired. I have a painting in my head, an angry painting red and yellow and gold bright, a woman lying, a body ravaged and vulnerable. My hair looks funny red and thick and straight and short. I thought it might look harsh. But my face is soft.

What story can I tell you that is my own? What story can I tell you without losing my body as I borrow the writing from it? What will you do with my story once it is told? Will you iron it out as well? Do you like my story?

I would like to write a love story, a story about love. It would be easier to write if I had purged everything but it's hard to throw up today. I would like to tell you a love story and I promise to tell it with a happy ending. I promise not to talk too much about throwing up. I promise not to make you uncomfortable. I promise not to tell.

* * *

In the bathroom I kill a cockroach as it tries to run past me. Your touch is familiar and always new. I have known your touch forever. One night you hold me very tight after replacing the telephone receiver in its cradle. My body is shaking I can't feel myself feeling you. I am crying and screaming. My voice is foreign and distant. I am curled into a ball. I cannot speak, the words on my body are in another language I cannot read I cannot see I am not there I am not coming back. Hold on you say I am here hold on tight. My hands reach out but not at you at myself trying to be rid of his words I pull my hair I scratch my face I draw blood his words are invading me taking over my body.

My fingers explore your body as I invent you with my touch. Your strong hands on my face your body soft and hard and close. You touch my breast carefully to see if your touch is welcome my nipple reaches for you I long to feel more of your closeness your stomach your chest your smile your eyes. My breasts hurt I am pregnant perhaps. Your touch is gentle. For a moment my sorrow fades and we are close and together.

* * *

I met you not so long ago. I meant to tell you that soon you would exist among the other marks on my body but the marks became noticeable and you did not need to be told. You are quiet sometimes you talk like an avalanche sometimes I look for words you do not have. I haven't told you that I am writing our love story. It is already written.

When I met you my body thin still not fully recovered from the anorexia you so different from him so quiet, ob-

21

serving me while I danced. I danced in your gaze, every move a result of the slow shifting of your eyes hesitating on my body. You sat all evening and I longed to sit close to you but my body fought to create distance. Your leg brushing against mine our eyes meeting I got up and danced until there was no more music and the dancers had found their places once more. You talked with me of mirrors, a conversation already deeply engraved in my memory as my body screamed out to yours. I have no mirrors. My reflection scares me like medusa, the recognition of myself my existence my pain and my joy. You saw the joy in my face because you saw me dancing.

I don't know when we first made love. Our bodies mould together. We have been making love ever since.

* * *

With you my anorexic body purged itself and grew and grew until I was so enormous I could no longer get through the door and I longed to know please tell me and lie if you want that you will be with me beside me together forever tell me you won't hurt me please don't leave.

* * *

Today I am lying on the couch. I have told my story before and I will tell it again and again until the pain subsides I will not throw up today I'm scared. I dream of a man in a red car a small car you run and chase me I am small and scared you catch me your hair bright red you empty me into a Glad garbage bag you throw me on the back of a truck I can't breathe I wake up my eyes are open I can see you I can't breathe I want to scream but the scream doesn't come here it is AAAAAAAAAHHHHHH I hear maman enter my room she holds me close shhhhh.

I long to turn around and look at you my analyst the one who is translating me into monsters and babies and mothers I want to know are you sleeping do you care are you listening? I am giving you my soul my spirit my body but I can't see you can I turn my head am I allowed? I want to be good. I am a good girl. I will be a success. The perfect analysand. I am afraid alone looking at the painting of the sea blue in front of me telling you about my dream, the dream with the doctors dressed all in blue. I am in maman's new apartment. The rooms are big with high ceilings, wood floors. A woman is there. She invites me to her friend's house that evening she leaves me the address. I go to the kitchen to get some food I don't want maman to see me. I leave maman's house I am looking for the friend's place. It is in a factory-like building, on the second floor. We enter a room. There is a door on either side. It looks like a psychiatric ward the doctors are dressed in blue. They let the other woman through but observe me for a long time. I am told to sit on a metal disk in an enclosure on the wall. I am naked under the hospital robe. The disk I am sitting on feels hot. I'm scared. The hall is like a pre-school with paintings and children's desks but there are no televisions.

Are you asleep? Do you sleep when I talk to you? Do you listen to me while I speak? Do you care? Do you want to hear my story? If you don't listen I will tell you a story about hatred and pain, not a love story. Please listen to me.

Analysis ends I pick up the pieces of myself that have fallen, the words left lying on the floor as they were discarded. I put my shoes on and walk into the slush outside. Summer will never come and you weren't listening I know I will throw up I need food I am scared. But you are there my lover waiting for me with the door open welcoming me your arms strong your heart open. Listen I say. Yes, you say. You listen as we drive in silence.

* * *

23

I am three years old living far away imagining Canada and dreaming about that place we have left behind and will return to one day. I am four years old we have returned but there is no red car in the driveway like the one I invented in my imagination and the people speak another language and maman is not there. Grandma tells me maman will be here soon and then you come and take me back to that place we left when I was big but you say I can't be big before I am small you don't know. The other girl my cousin is prettier blue eyes blond hair smiling I want my hair like hers short no braids. Papa says yes and we cut it but I am not as pretty always so slow says my aunt like a turtle says maman. I listen I can hear them but they don't hear me. Maman spells the words you talk for hours on the telephone it is not polite to interrupt you say but I want to say I know the words you spell o-n-i-o-n I don't like them you will put them in the sauce you don't think I have understood but I know and they remind me of snakes.

I am not pretty short red-blond hair straight-curly so serious and slow I can't run fast I always get caught first when we play hide-and-seek. I got ten dollars you tell me you have a good report card I am sad no dollars for me papa tells me one of the faces on my report was not smiling you had ten smiling ones nine for me. I cry but you don't see because I am big and I hide my tears.

Today I am big no longer five or four or three and I have many smiling faces when I walk in the street and greet those who look at me. Then I come home and take off my face and throw up. I have no mirrors. The music moves inside me I can feel the cello as Charpentier holds open the door to the cathedral. The stained-glass windows glimmer in the sliver of sunlight that enters with me. Your voice envelops me you sing to me and my face softens falls to the ground and then I am there me.

I am six today and papa has left but I don't ask. Every morning my little brother looks for him I see tears in maman's eyes. I look at her hands. They always shake now. I don't ask. It is my birthday and I see there is a gift from you. I want to be alone, open it slowly find you again papa où es-tu? A xylophone a book a card I read it again and again a picture on the front of a man in pencil climbing papa où es-tu? Maman cries and I hold her. I am seven today.

* * *

You come to see me in my apartment the one I share with maman. You arrive late sorry to be late to pick up shirts. I see you come before you are there I feel your body next to mine starved. You sit in front of me on the floor your legs extended watching. I talk always so many stories in my head you do not know me. Through the window on top of the bed I can see the office buildings. With every hour a new floor lights up sometimes goes dark and disappears. You come to look and I move away. Our bodies long to touch but I have forgotten how to touch to feel I move away. Sometimes you are quiet and we listen to one-another breathe and then I talk again because the silence exposes me I am vulnerable are you leaving? I'm cold you are still here the sun has not yet come up you must work in the morning are we falling in love? All of the floors are lit now there is a grey tint to the October sky it will snow soon I think. I am cold the floor is hard I want to take a bath hot water against my skin I walk down the stairs with you and you leans against the light pink walls I am perched on the last step the sun is rising I can see it from the window in the hall we don't know how to say good-bye. We still don't know how to say goodbye.

   Last night we slept next to one-another and when I had a nightmare you tried to wake me. I couldn't wake up my sleep ravaged by memories my body shaking. Last night I fell asleep first I woke the light still on you were holding me tight your arms strong around me folding my body into yours. I can feel time printing you onto my skin. Our bodies entwined we fit you are close you do not know my memories but you cry.

I am scared in analysis. I am facing her I want to run do you find me interesting will you stay do you care? You listen and interrupt sometimes your conversation involved and enthusiastic I think you understand. I come home and throw up.

My painting is eating me up. I have tried to swallow the world but instead it is devouring me leaving impenetrable scars. The canvas is large big as my wall the paint goes on thickly red, black, skin. The painting skin is being dripped on erased my body is disappearing. On the balcony my hibiscus tree is blooming three flowers fourteen blooms beautiful alive. I watch the flowers feel the sun hot on my head my shoulders my legs the rest of me covered because I am enormous so big full. From my window I look into their apartments I watch the television they are cooking dinner making love. I am alone in my apartment a place of my own no longer with maman but not always alone because you come sometimes and we lie on the bed red and yellow and orange we make love our bodies fit together writing a language of our own.

* * *

The Gateway

"Behold this gateway, dwarf!" I continued. "It has two faces. Two paths meet here; no one has yet followed either to its end. This long lane stretches back for an eternity. And the long lane out there, that is another eternity. They contradict each other, these paths, they offend each other face to face; and it is here at this gateway that they come together. The name of the gateway is inscribed above: "Moment.""

All that is straight lies, says the dwarf, all truth is crooked I think as I enter into my apartment. I haven't been here since yesterday, yesterday's vomit still hanging in the air, unfinished painting on the kitchen wall red black bleeding.

Through the gateway I enter and choose you your smell. I do not smell the vomit I smell your skin sweat clinging cool wet. I long for you my body turns toward you but you are not there. This moment is mine. I clean the vomit for the last time.

I can tell you a story would you like to hear my dream the one about the volcano? I will tell you do you want to know will you hear do you listen? In my dream I am climbing into a tree house so high I might die it is dangerous papa tells me to keep climbing I must climb I can do it I will show him I am big I am strong I will show him I climb I am tired I almost fall before I arrive at the top. From the tree house I can see to the other side of the river. I see a valley deep and red. I turn to warn him but he does not listen. I am scared. I run to help I must save the people I must tell them the volcano is approaching they might die I must save them but as soon as I've gathered them the red hot lava stops just one meter. I wake hot the sun shining through your window house cluttered with bits of you and you hold me.

* * *

And this slow spider, which crawls in the moonlight, and this moonlight itself, and I and you in the gateway, whispering together, whispering of eternal things – must not all of us have been there before? And return and walk in that other lane, out there, before us, in this long dreadful lane – must we not eternally return?

My brother and I are little already big, grownups first and then children and soon we will grow up again. We live on a farm sometimes a big house with two staircases one from the kitchen up to my bedroom and to the bathroom the other staircase from the living room up to his room and to my parents' bedroom. Later when my sister is born the second staircase leads up to her room as well. Now everything has changed. My room is their room (she and papa) and hers is no longer hers and I don't know where he sleeps when he comes.

He always wakes early a quiet child and looks into my room his brown eyes wide we slither down the stairs the paint peeling dark red into the kitchen not yet renovated. White toast and corn-syrup in the red bowl with the side that reaches up and stops spilling the one for babies but I am not a baby I am big. Shhhh or maman will hear and she will be angry she doesn't like messes we are quiet she won't know. She always does. He goes out to play mounds of sand his groundhog friend by his side alone until the sun falls he is little so old already. When she is born she is different makes noise and doesn't care if maman knows I watch her in awe. I bring her into the world tired maman asleep again having a baby is work cleaning the house dirt everywhere. I will clean up don't worry go to sleep I will feed her I say. I look at her small in her cradle so different. She climbs onto his knees wants to be kissed and he holds her tight adorable with her curly head. We the old ones watch because we cannot move onto his lap we are invisible quiet he does not see us. She is loud screaming.

Driving again. The car is quiet. Maman and papa in front and we three in the back two of us pretending to sleep holding our breath they are not fighting not talking. He stops the car outside the neon sign I see it shining and I hold my breath perhaps they will smile sshhhhh. This is their moment. I extend my arms and form a gateway they can't see me I am invisible. She orders cherry and he says the same and they look at each other could they be smiling? Me too screams the little one. My gateway falls, the moment is gone. Shhhhh.

* * *

This is a love story, a story about love.

* * *

I am three years old we are far away still in that place before the house of my imagination with the red car and the long driveway. The house is still. My room is big with shutters green and a balcony my bed against the wall. The night invades my room I am scared raboo will eat me look he bit me my hand my skin look! I close my eyes I hold my breath perhaps you won't come tonight stay away go away please maman. It is Christmas and my present is big so big there is a bow no wrapping paper. A baby carriage. I am big enough to have a baby today. I am three.

Last night I screamed in my sleep again. You held me close and gently caressed my skin. Shhhhh.

* * *

In my book there is a picture of you. You do not recognize yourself. I have painted you black spray paint body skin ravaged mirror shards. You do not look you do not come to see. When I paint you my stomach aches my eyes are tired. My body is painting you.

You turn from the painting hold me in your arms I feel your hardness touching me bodies meeting. In the kitchen my painting is growing shards of glass on the head body broken pain. I approach my painting with anger I long for the closeness of your body I long for you your touch this painting is scaring me I am scared what is emerging from me what is my creation who am I?

Last night I am chased by my dream I wake in terror raped again my body shaking my eyes dry did I say no I don't remember.

We are in the hospital together I am waiting for my turn soon they will tell me am I pregnant. I sit next to you my lover you read a magazine your arm draped over my shoulder. I am laughing I show you Ann Landers can you believe it I say but your face doesn't look you aren't listening I turn away. Listen you say. You take my hand and begin to read. You read of a woman who writes her writing strong her body on the page imprinted in its anger. You cry as you read my eyes are dry. You are crying my tears feeling my pain. My body is numb. I hear about a life shattered about a man and a little girl and years and success and a broken heart you read me she writes me. The nurse calls my name. Your features marked and tired you stop reading and I leave.

This morning we have breakfast together we go there often it is our place. They like to feed our tired bodies still drowsy from the night we like to sit and watch the people as they walk by. I order for you and you nod we sit to-gether side by side pushing the seats next to one-another. I think of an afternoon together in Montreal waiting for the plane sitting in a café watching. She is fabulous look at her dress bright eyes we laugh. Your arm tight around mine we look at the her grace enraptured. Today we have breakfast together. We watch but we don't look. We are waking up still discovering one another. You hold your food with one hand me with the other kiss my mouth full of food. We are lovers I know your body when I go to sleep at night I must discover it anew every morning. Hello this is me do you want to touch come here stay close, hello.

* * *

You look at me. I have no mirrors you are my mirror. You conceive me with your eyes you are my existence I am you. You bring me into the world you create me. I am you where are my words I have no words you must speak through my mouth. I want to write to paint to live I can-not paint until you give me the colour what colour will I choose tell me who I am.

I am six years old a little girl blue-green eyes watchful. I draw pictures of the place I have not yet seen write sto-ries that invent me. I am a queen I have never lived here listen and I will tell you who I am please tell me who I am. I am six years old I write myself into my book the book that stays hidden from your eyes the book that tells me that I am a writer the book you can't see the book without words. You ask me about the book but I tell no secrets. I cannot write for you. I write to keep myself hidden. I can-not expose myself through my writing. I write and write and write but I will not let you see because these aren't your words I am writing.

I live without mirrors alone in my imagination. You are my mirror and you and you. Tell me how to look, how to smile. My painting bleeds with open mirrors, images you can't see, reflections of yourself. The hands cover my body and I hide but it is no longer me who is hiding you have disappeared I am free of you I am free. My painting tears my stomach explosives dynamite my stomach ulcer churns and I break out into a sweat. I run from my words to myself to my paint running still I am scared by my reflection terrified by my creation. The painting is glazed, contained within its fragments. The body of my painting turns into mountains into body blood and gold. Violent splendour calling out to you to look to be struck by the beauty of destruction you have ravaged me.

Today I am old twenty-five and a thousand and I live in a place with no mirrors. Today I paint a reflection of myself I paint myself I write my book for the first time. You are beautiful you said today I am beautiful violent enraged. Today I write my book and I let you see I tell you it's a love story I don't tell you about the edges of the broken mirrors like the one that leaves a gash in my hand. Today I let you read. In the jarred mirror you see me see yourself.

* * *

Analysis again I sit in front of you and look away. I think of a story. It is a story about Care an ancient fable. When Care crosses the river she sees some clay takes a piece and begins to shape it. Jupiter arrives and Care asks him to give it spirit. For the spirit he bestows upon the creature he requests his name. Care holds strong and denies him the naming of her creation. Earth arrives and desires that her name be conferred onto the creation since she furnished it with part of her body. They ask Saturn to be the arbiter and he decides that Jupiter will receive its spirit after death and Earth its body. But since it was Care that first shaped it she will possess it as long as it lives.

I create myself. The analyst sits before me. I am quiet. You are listening listening to my silence I know I can speak you will not name me you will let me name myself.

I am not ready to be named. I have no other name than my own which I keep for myself. It is a gift I will not share. I begin to speak you listen your eyes open looking at me and seeing. Tell me about the painting you say and I describe the body hidden dark and the gold hands the lustre of the gloss on the acrylic shards of mirror. You have destroyed them have broken the mirrors your pain is yours you say. My book I say the book is stabbing me hurting pulling yes you say. Today analysis tomorrow and again. My day is structured paint words images talk analysis read make love. I miss you, my love. Yesterday I wrote about you today I am writing about me but soon you shall return, soon my love. You look at me I play with the curl on my forehead red and look at you I don't know what to say I am scared I won't throw up today I'm scared.

Cherries one after the other red juicy stain on my white shirt soft against my skin. I walk through the market one more cherry then a cappuccino strong sweet with frothed milk the sun shining high. Summer flowers and vegetables people everywhere exposed sun shining in their faces. I look for you among the crowd I don't see you I walk slowly small steps ignore the man making lewd comments fuck you fuck you fuck you. I smile my mask is on you cannot see me it is not me you are looking at. I walk by your house you are not home I know gone for the week I want to see you maman to have you close to me you are not there. I am old twenty-five and a thousand and I have crossed under the gateway that is called moment. Time exists inside me I have swallowed it up I want to tell you I want to show you you are not there. I walk up to smell your smell it has left as well. You are gone.

The glaze is dry painting finished you have raped me I have painted you can you see you look are those mountains you ask where is the body? So beautiful the painting red and gold and black body underneath exposed vulnerable invisible.

All truth is crooked said the dwarf, time itself a circle. Zarathustra listens. I have swallowed time. I am a circle standing under the gateway called moment.

* * *

The Dancer

My heels twitched, then my toes hearkened to understand you, and rose: for the dancer has his ears in his toes.

Breakfast buns with raisins with cheese, cherries and sweet mangoes. The sun strong and bright another summer morning the market shines you are gone I am alone. Last night you entered into my place stood in front of my painting watched me out of the corner of your eye, me the creator of pain. You move like a cat slithering away from me onto my balcony you look at the red hibiscus. On the small bed we lie on top of one-another hands wandering looking for lost skin left untouched for the day. You are here again my love. I missed you.

This morning you drop me off to face another day alone with my words. I will miss you but I have many stories to tell. Come back soon. And listen.

The market alive with bright flowers the cherries explode in my mouth not on my white dress still pure white sheer outline showing in the sun.

I meet you today for the second time our bodies have not yet touched I long to reach out to you. Four years I have protected my body. Four years I have starved myself. I exist for no one not even me.

I remember your breasts against mine aggressive. You will not hurt me why do you hurt me no! stop! please! Your body angry against mine clothes strewn on the ground hands everywhere I cry out your hand on my mouth.

I meet you today for the second time your eyes penetrate me your gaze drawing us in there is so much you do not know. We stand across from one-another the pool cue heading for the blue one you sink it your graceful form leaning against the pool table. Your face is serious your forehead wrinkled in concentration you miss it's my turn you move toward me your body close to mine my heart beating fast. I cannot concentrate I miss. Your body approaches mine your leg rubs against my thigh as you position yourself for the next shot. I didn't know pool was a seducer's game.

* * *

The air thick with summer today my white dress billowing in the wind I am eight years old blue shorts and a red shirt. The farm is my stage I walk along the gravel road the camera following me stories on my path. I live to tell my stories. The boy in my class I write him into my story he is waiting for me perhaps in that city far away almost two more months before summer ends and September comes. Reporters follow me what do you think they ask your voice is vital to our story they say. I answer their questions slowly I speak to one reporter at a time please don't interrupt me I say it's impolite wait until I'm f-i-n-i-s-h-e-d.

I am dancing today I have my dancing shoes on tied to my toes would you like to dance you promised me a dance. We have not yet danced together you watched me dance now it's our turn would you like to dance? We make supper together noodles orange and green broccoli my broccoli in your noodles you laugh and we make love.

The pool game is finished we take our coats the wind is cold no snow yet. The others leave the world is empty we are alone would you like to take my hand would you like me to drive you home you ask? The car keeps us separate time to think to look the other we will never really know I feel fear mounting inside my body I do not want to be alone not yet no not home I say let's go somewhere else a drink perhaps? The Manx Pub is dark we hold each other tight faces touching lips meeting who are you what lips are these my body is flying into your arms hold on! You do not say a word the hours pass the pub closes around us we are the only ones in the world we are invisible they are invisible we have nothing to say too many questions. Tonight we are alone together.

* * *

The summer is still here it is not September yet. I have a friend she shows me magazines naked women men strange stories my heart beats faster I don't want to be caught where did you find these? You tell me to take off my clothes you say that it is hot. I take off my blue shorts white underwear. Your breasts are bigger you cover them in cheap lace take off skirt blouse underwear your body longer than mine you are a woman I am a child so old already more than a thousand years. You tell me a story a man by the church rips off your clothes hits you red mark on your neck pain blood. I watch horror growing inside me come here you say you show me pictures look at this one how do you feel you're so pretty come here. I am hungry I want to go home your body heavy on top of mine I am small I can't breathe kiss me you say. Feel your body you say do you feel it so hot under mine? My heart is beating your breasts soft on my cheeks black hair tickling my stomach I am invisible no one can see me. I dance you turn on the music lie on your bed watch me move to *The Bay City Rollers* I dance I forget your breast against my face your lips your body moving against mine faster and faster I dance.

* * *

The end of the night is here you take me home you are gentle my body afraid of your touch will I invite you up? You do not ask we both know soon we will be lovers tonight I want my bed to myself. We sit in the car afraid to talk you calm me silent who are you I want to ask goodbye I say. Will you come to see me soon you ask Saturday? Yes I say I will come I cannot stay away from you I am losing my body it is yours but I do not tell you it is my secret. I walk up the stairs leaving you behind I hear your car the sun is coming up. Quietly I turn the key in the lock he and maman are sleeping I slide into my bed my body alive with your magic weighted down by your silence.

It is Saturday I drive to that place where the magic grows where you live in the junkyard of your life cars and tools and wood and cans. I arrive my hands in my pockets body still thin traces of anorexia red pants black shirt hair long red curly watching. You are not alone I see him in the other room I stand on the jeep frame in the middle of your kitchen floor I am on a trapeze look I am flying will you fly away with me? You kiss me gently on the lips eggs on the stove breakfast in the afternoon. We do not talk you eat I watch you lay down my books on the cold floor Heidegger in the middle of your clutter frenetically calm. I am reading must give a presentation talk about Care. In every word I see your face I read you as you appear in every sentence breaking the words being-towards-you, alongside-you, being-in-the-you-world-you-you-you. You do not look at me you work upstairs you are distant he is here as well working on a door there are three of us here we are not alone I am cold hungry night has fallen where are you where am I are you here? It is late he leaves are you hungry you ask. We drive to a pub there are two of them they sing a man and woman from Wales she plays the piano I sit next to you you are quiet we eat in silence. The night envelops us I am in your arms I don't remember when we first make love we make love all night we fall asleep we wake our bodies entwined in silence. Morning shines through the small window cold air blowing in I go to the bathroom peel your body from mine we are separate once more. The steps are cold on my bare feet the bathroom is downstairs through the kitchen I walk on the frame trapeze I am flying I am sinking. In your arms I speak to you but you cannot hear me a thousand questions I ask will you hurt me who are you can you love? You your body different from mine different different you are not you.

On the way home I cry tears flooding the car the ride long Suzanne Vega loud. We will never speak again I am sure so quiet no more words you cannot see me I do not exist in your eyes do you see me here I am I am here here here here! I write you a letter I cannot be with you I write I am scared can you love how much pain have you suffered how deep are the gashes? Don't tell me who you have loved before tell me who you can love do you rape will you cut me hit me tie me up in knots will you speak to me will you hurt me will you destroy me will I still exist when you leave?

* * *

The summer is ending I leave the reporters behind I climb the long driveway alone. We have a contract for you they said you will be famous come with us tell us your stories we will take you away. It is a lie I know because I made you up you cannot have me you exist only through my words. I will dance for you I tell them and I dance for them for their eyes. Through their cameras they look at me I am here they see me dance. I am the camera.

You will not touch me again strange smells breasts black pubic hair wet. Summer is over. She is so nice maman says be nice to her I won't don't be so immature maman says she likes you. The summer ends we pack our bags they are fighting again pack she says clean up he says I don't hear them we are going home summer is finally over I can't wait. The house in the city smells the same every year it waits for us I enter my room yellow soft it is expecting me my bed my smell my things summer is over. In my room I play the music loud in my head and dance body swaying to my sound so loud so soft I fall onto my bed and cry summer is over.

* * *

You write to me tell me about love your letter gentle your words strong. Love is not something we have not something we give not something we take away it is who we are it moves with us as we are moved by it you say. Love exists as a part of my being you say I love and will do anything for those I love anything I consider appropriate. Am I appropriate? I read your words again and again print them out copy them read them live them you exist you have spoken. I am alive through your words. Do you know about the demonic I want to ask, about Kierkegaard about inclosing reserve and unfree disclosure? Do you know about desire? Yes I say silently. I know.

I am exploding with words my body erupting you have entered me I am bleeding I am alive. I want to speak to you listen to me I want to speak. I desire you I desire your desire I desire my desire. I take out my paints it is late I paint my words on my wall bright orange leaking gold stars blue glitter fingerprints. I write you a story I tell you I am a writer I know you say how do you know? You are a writer you say and you wrap your body around mine. Through the window they see us close they know we are together there is no room for them we are lovers.

Flowers blooming on my hibiscus three of them my tree growing my balcony hot with the noon summer sun shining strong. Red telephone beside me quiet the city humming outside. I speak with you on the phone again

today you the one who introduced me to my lover the
night of the wedding last summer. Last time I saw you
you reminded me of Jesus I've never met him I am not
religious I discovered him once in a picture I was seven
the grownups wouldn't let me look they could not find
him but I saw. Sometimes grown-ups forget to open their
eyes. That night at the wedding I saw your striped pants
yellow shirt you did not come near me I was alone plat-
form soles black dress sunglasses alone. There was no
music no dancing my feet leaden with small-talk longing to approach you. Cold evening falling I changed into
black leggings arms cool in the night wind I stood in
front of the bonfire alone. You came and sat next to me
your presence gentle you brought your guitar. I turned
around opened my eyes the circle big suddenly many
people singing the fire high and red. You sang were shy
didn't want to play your guitar you passed it to the other
one he played it well asked us what we wanted to sing I
whispered my choice you didn't hear me. I wanted to sing
with you didn't want to leave with maman come with me
she said I can drive you home you said you remind me of
Jesus your blond hair long body tall and thin bare feet
and sandals. The bride and groom left car covered with
shaving cream relieved I think that it was over no more
weddings and we sat in the car next to one-another. On
the way home you took me to him.

We built another fire the night long and cool and red
and hot I hadn't been out so late I had been sick four years
eight years twelve years anorexia. Your friend I saw him
lean toward me he looked at me and saw he smiled you
will be my lover someday I thought. I should have taken
you straight home you thought but you said nothing.

I like you you are not my lover you are my friend your
heart aches the voice in the labyrinth of emotions so
sweet.

* * *

I am eight years old and I love to dance. My words dance on the page as I create you you exist as I write you down. My words are my lovers you invent me with your touch I dance you under the moon until the sun comes up bright orange. I am eight years old and the school year is beginning I have wiped you off my skin the summer is over. My room smells of September the walls pale yellow the bed wet under my tears. Tomorrow school and I will not tell you I will not talk about the reporters who listened me on the long driveway at the farm I will not tell you my story there are no words for you.

I dance after you, I follow you wherever your traces linger. Where are you? Give me your hand! Or only one finger!

Zarathustra speaks he loves to dance will you dance with me Zarathustra?

* * *

The Symphony

Today I write a symphony for you the cello moaning at my side. Listen. The words short and staccato viola playing clarinet and flute soft melody of the piano are you listening?

Her voice fills the room she sings Charpentier the cathedral ringing her soprano magic my apartment alive with her music.

End of the session analysis over for today I am tired numb my eyelids are drooping will you hold me tonight? The symphony has fallen onto itself the tones dissonant the echoes inside need tuning. You approach me carefully haven't seen me in a day your lips press against mine my body limp. I cannot reach you my instrument is silent I have no words left there is no music inside me. We lie next to one-another you talk I listen your silence broken by a new passion tell me more I am tired writing is burning my soul have you seen my painting?

What are you writing she asks analysis long today. Are you writing the music that you can't hear are you writing the words that will allow you to speak? Yes, I think yes yes. I am writing my body I am writing my soul I am writing my music I say but I forget to speak and you don't hear me. My imagination is my truth the truth that doesn't exist the truth that changes every time I hear a new note every time the bow moves the cello and the stained glass windows catch a ray of sunlight.

I am little I am big I am twenty-five and a thousand and they ask is it true did it happen that way how was it can you repeat it are you sure it was really that way? I am little I am big I am two and a thousand and they ask is it true did it happen that way how was it can you repeat it are you sure it was really that way? I don't know I am screaming the words caught in my throat. Memory doesn't exist I exist as I create myself the creation is hurting stop it hurts please stop stop! In analysis I tell you I don't know I will perhaps never know I am tired of trying to know what I will never know. Does it exist? Did it happen? I don't know I don't know I don't know. Yes of course it happened look at me I am here I am writing I am talking to you look at me! Do you see the gash on my left breast look closer you cannot see it it is hidden behind the skin it is there. I made that gash I placed it there in memory of you and you and you. You did not harm me I harmed myself in memory of you.

I am three years old I am little my body light under the white sheet middle of the afternoon maman is gone I don't like to sleep in the afternoon. I am two and a thousand. You enter my room big voice hard my body trembles. You sit on my bed stroke my head push into my mouth I gag I refuse to eat I am big now I have a baby carriage I am old enough to have a baby your body heavy on mine.

Last night you hold me my lover your body cool with sweat mosquitoes flying around your head body itchy. You hold me my body aching with memory stomach pain breasts sore. Your touch is gentle your caress tender go to sleep you say can you sleep? I am tired I cannot sleep did it happen do you know will I know?

* * *

I am three years old little I am having a baby my baby is black plastic he has a penis can you see maman? I am two years old two and a thousand I sit on the balcony body hunched over I cannot sleep nightmares coming in through my shutters. Outside my door suitcases she is leaving I am alone I am three she is crying where are you going maman? I do not speak will not swallow my food will not let you inside will not open my mouth will not tell you my secret.

In my book I write my body the body that holds your imprint the one I have painted etched in gold with red black paint mirror shards. You still exist I do not see you I know you are there I remember do you remember?

My lover's hand on your imprint startles me the hand tracing you removing you lifting you off my skin. My heart is revealed red bloody vulnerable dangerous.

* * *

The human body is not a thing or a substance, given, but a continuous creation.

We play in a tree house I am eight years old there are four of us you the other girl and the two boys the one I like. You spin the bottle take off your clothes you say yes I say naked you laugh. What is a slut I ask maman why she asks.

Maman makes me a halter top matching shorts terry cloth pink blue and white I love it wear it to school. Velcro on the back the school bully undoes it holds me down come and see they say come and see her breasts! I have no breasts don't look at me don't rip my halter top maman made it. You send me to the principle's office it is your fault you say go home and change you say halter tops are forbidden. I am eight years old tell me maman why don't they like me how can I be more like them tell me. Change your clothes you say you will not be like them you are different I am not going back I say no you say.

This is not a symphony they cannot hear the music they are calling me names I will not hear them I cannot hear the music my ears are deaf.

* * *

John Zorn is breaking my symphony stop! no! stop! Symphony broken into fragments exploding dissonance cello out of tune the warning on the CD says do not listen for extended periods of time can cause ear damage glass falling breaking my body. I have fallen I am broken I am walking on broken glass feet bleeding I am walking on my hands upside down where am I going?

We meet again you have invited many people wearing costumes night darkening. You are there my lover dressed in black intoxicated by the night and beer that will make your head spin your stomach churn but you don't think of that now. You let me in I am with him the one who introduced me to you you look at me you do not see me. The music is loud the dance floor vibrant with our movement. I cannot see you you are not there you are not here you do not come to dance with me. You disappear all in black I am laughing be careful they say as they watch you fly into the darkness alone. You glide toward me own me with your kiss leave again all in black my cape swinging on the dance floor body alive I am a symphony my feet have healed no broken glass my body whole. You take out a guitar we sing you are asleep passed out from the alcohol dead night. Look they say he does not care I cannot wake you I do not try. I watch you in your sleep face unrevealing mouth open drowned in your intoxication. The one who tells me to be careful to stay away from you puts me to sleep rubs my back tells me to forget about you I pretend to be asleep then I sneak up on you and watch you in your dreams so distant. You wake eyes cloudy mouth dry do you recognize me I want to ask do you remember me? They told me to leave to let you go I say why are you here you ask. I don't know.

I return to school eight years old my body broken by your touch loose shirt long and unrevealing no Velcro.

* * *

Sky white translucent high humidity sweltering heat your blinds are drawn I cannot look into your window. The air in my apartment still only my hands moving on the keyboard my stomach purging words one after the other. I switch you off "Canticum ad Beatam Virginem Mariam" turn to Bill Frisell "Have a Little Faith" yes music loud no more baroque sounds screaming off my walls floorboards creaking. The disk is yellow some say it isn't music I hear it in my heart fragmented making me whole tearing me apart.

My dress sticks to my back sweat pouring down my stomach through the white lace body suit. I want to wear my white dress naked underneath I can't you say I must protect myself from the ones who cannot restrain themselves. The shimmer of my body breast under white dress makes them crazy it is my fault if I tempt them.

I write in fragments filling the page with my body restrained when I try to write your words big words long sentences where is the order you ask what happened next? and then? Listen to my language. It is a symphony.

* * *

My stomach is full I want to throw up pieces of undigested food fragments strewn on the toilet bowl the undigested remnants of my pain. I talk to you my sentences incomplete I am alone the world is big is this fiction you ask?

I want to throw up fiction undigested truth I cannot tell you I am fiction what is truth? The fragments of my symphony left unfinished by my side my desire created by your absence the absence of myself the absence of my fiction. I am my story I am telling you my fiction stop asking for the truth!

Analysis begins she asks me how I will tell my story will I invent myself fragmented always distant from myself always a performance? Perhaps I say my story is always different it changes every day it is pain and joy the pain strong today. I want to throw up. These words leave marks on the page traces of myself can you see me? I want to dance to sing to listen to the symphony the volume is low my body silent words heavy and lifeless today.

I am nine years old nightmares every night tears are you leaving abandoning me (a word I learn much later) are you there? I sing myself to sleep at night waiting for your kiss sometimes you come so late I lie awake waiting. You peer inside my door you see my eyes wide open you are awake you say yes I say will you kiss me goodnight? You come toward me lay down sometimes beside me rub my back a little mon ange you say and kiss me. I sing at night before I fall asleep as I wait for your kiss.

I scream in my sleep another nightmare he is sitting on me I am trapped I cannot breathe I am scared maman! You lie beside me wipe my forehead gently later the little one will have nightmares as well and you will hold her tight. She is not born yet I am your only daughter you hold me tight of course you say I will be here tomorrow we will be here together a family.

You think I am asleep you return to your bed the one you share with papa I follow you and watch as you crawl in we are together I watch your body close to his I cannot go back to sleep I am scared will you be there in the morning?

Today we are not together this is not truth and you did not abandon me. I know the fears of childhood I understand them still feel them in that scar the one I drew on my left breast. I will not throw up I tell myself I can resist. I am the culprit. I am twenty-five and a thousand and I am the bearer of my pain. They will not abandon me I will abandon myself to pay them back. How foolish.

Today I write a symphony and if you want I will include you what do you play? These are my words this is my music we will play it for me we will play it on my body as the words are tattooed onto my skin. You can play loud or soft but be careful soon this will be your story too you will see the trace of your fingertips hidden in that crease on my stomach, on the curve of my breast.

* * *

Twenty Shirts

Twenty shirts clean you pick them up pile them in the back of your car clutchless needing repair. The car lurches forward as you start it without the clutch you move into traffic drive me home back to my book waiting for my fingers itching to write. Ten thousand words I have written ten thousand words from my body written for you a love story the story of my life.

Your shirts are clean piled plastic on the back seat of your car my dirty laundry piling up basket overflowing. I have been writing five days five chapters I will write twenty-five years of my life. My white dress soiled I am not clean my fingers itchy for the keyboard I will not take time to change. When you read this I will have changed.

They look at me don't see me do not recognize me do not know who I am do not understand my words. When we are around them you hold me close protect me from their disinterest without you I am alone in this maze they cannot understand.

Twenty shirts plastic covered on the back seat of your car you must be clean they tell you we pay you for your cleanliness. Every day you go to them clean shirt clean body hours in an office with no walls. They give you money you are rich your time is expensive they pay you for your time. No one pays me for my time it is worth so much that I have no money to pay the rent. No shirts clean in the back of my car no car my fingers alive letters peeling off my body blue red orange.

Black and white pictures developing in the darkroom of my imagination I smell eggs cooking through the open window they cannot see me their blinds are drawn. Some mornings I hear them moan in ecstasy as they reach orgasm this morning the smell of eggs and coffee have they already made love? Mornings are for making love you say afternoons as well I am too tired in the evening wake me up. Their eggs fill my apartment they don't invite me over they are closed off to the world the world of lovers I see him through my window the man with the long black dreads. Pictures black and white of me and you lovers naked in my room most of them unfocused one of them strange the camera looking up picture of my underbreast swollen tummy am I pregnant? The picture of you the one I love you are sitting on my bed body turned toward me you are beautiful. I will paint you this picture will grow you will invade me I will create you black and white on my canvas with spots of colour.

I turn off the music my apartment silent only the sound of my fingers as they hit the keys. For you my lover I will keep everything I write. I will send you these words one by one you can read them savour them this is a story for you this is a story about love.

* * *

I am nine years old I have nightmares still sometimes the fighting stops today you tell me you are pregnant. You walk around maman growing stomach revealed majestic like a queen red shorts with polka-dots brown bikini top. You lean into the garden pull weeds they stop to look at you you are beautiful. Your body long and lithe stomach dark brown tan it is the summer I am watching you. Come help me in the garden you say this time you do not force me you know I like to be alone you are gentle this year the baby in your stomach makes you dream. He leans toward you do you need anything he asks I have not seen him so gentle with you. Sometimes he admires you in the mirror look at her back he tells me so long and graceful she is beautiful your mother. My brother is not here in my memory I don't remember him he is playing alone I think he is alone all of the time a lonely boy. You grow your stomach exploding cheeks glowing you are strong.

The baby comes she is ugly brown tattoo on her upper lip not a tattoo you say a birth mark it will go away. We go and look at her through the glass you are safe from us who are you? Maman stays there eats sugar pie peanut brittle you will never come home you like it there it is quiet.

Baby at home maman tired baby screaming hungry all the time throwing up on your shoulder. I take the baby in my arms you are mine I think I am pregnant you are my baby. Maman feeds you breasts full of milk I have no milk I change your dirty diapers rock you you scare me eyes so confidant demanding.

Today I am twenty-five and a thousand I will not have a baby I have already given birth I was ten I was two and a thousand she came out of your stomach you are mine. My stomach swells I am enormous it is your imagination the doctor says my imagination is pregnant. Today my breasts hard and sore expecting you the one who will be my child my words my book my painting. I will feed you with the milk from my breasts I will feed myself.

The baby grows locks and a smile everyone watches. Later she will cry at night for a year scared of the darkness scared of me. I am your mother I gave birth to you through maman's stomach I gave you my body and now I am dying and you are afraid. All winter you wait for me I am in hospital starving I do not eat the pain is growing you can feel my pain we are attached our bond still strong our bond broken.

Today you are big older than me sometimes you look at me still guarded afraid. I am alive I tell you they have untied us we are detached your eyes cloud up tears flow down your beautiful cheeks your beauty resplendent. I invite you for breakfast pancakes with strawberries you sit in front of me sticky with maple syrup you look at me. I cannot avert my gaze your rich brown eyes hair long brown curly lips thick luscious. I have not created you I think you are not mine you are safe you live apart your world separate I miss you you are gone.

* * *

I can hear the rain falling on the ground I am high off the ground I cannot see it it is in my ears. The dirty laundry still waits for me the morning is passing time is disappearing eaten up by my words.

You speak to me tell me about love say that it exists inside you I am melting I am disappearing you have swallowed me up. I am looking to you my lover I am looking for an answer from you I want to know I want to feel your love I want to be you I am losing my mind. I move away from you I have known you but a few months I am allowing you to be me I have opened my heart to you I am losing myself I am afraid.

The man downstairs sells me a drink I gulp it down with the straw forget to breathe gasp for air it is not very sweet my stomach full of cherries. My fingers are blue cherry stains staining my words staining the truth that is my fiction. My stomach cherry tree watered by my fizzling drink I am drowning overflowing flooded by my body. I throw away the cherry seeds. I swallowed them when I was little maman said be careful a cherry tree will grow in your stomach it has grown I don't want to swallow them anymore. I reach into my stomach pluck a cherry I must be careful I might remove my heart bruised by the memory of how I almost gave it away.

I hadn't known you long my lover you said to me keep your heart I will not give you mine we will learn to love our hearts intact. The painting on my wall mad with exhaustion you look at it say this is your heart your mind keep it it is yours. What is mine? You stay a minute. Silent you watch me. I have spent three days in bed my eyes alight with madness and crazy dreams. For three days I have fought with your love for three days I have been alone. I do not tell you my fear the madness that invades me the darkness inside. You lift my shirt press your lips gently against the curve of my stomach I love you you say you are the darkness you are the madness you are the beauty you are the joy the light you you. Your words make me shake I am trembling I can see my skin flying from my body words bouncing off the walls hold on you say hold on. You take my hand and lead me home. My heart is not mine.

The painting on my wall fades a little my skin is returning to my body words shaky I take your hand and speak my desire once more.

* * *

I am eleven I am twelve you are growing curls extending from your forehead red cheeks you are teething screaming hungry desiring. She is tired our mother the one who feeds you my little one. The sky has fallen the peace is broken he is angry they are fighting. I shelter you my little one make you my own adopt you in the cherry fields of my imagination. She escapes often hidden in her own world I will take care of things maman don't worry. Maman rests her tired body on my shoulder weary from life she goes out to find her world she leaves me with our body. The little one is now mine I will be her mother I will glue them back together we will be a family I will sew them up as they come apart.

You are mine you no longer need maman's breast my breast is empty I cannot feed you you will not eat my food. I don't tell them you are mine. Sometimes you scream little one you are confused you have two mothers. My breast is empty you are mine I feed you with my flesh you are my body.

I look down I see the scars on my stomach I have borne a child I have populated the world can you see them no they are invisible bright red to my eyes. You were my child grew from me tore yourself away look there is a crack in my heart where the cord is severed.

I wonder if I am pregnant.

* * *

The test is negative I am not pregnant you were never my child I did not conceive you. My breasts are sore still full of milk you never drank from me I am still waiting. My body expectant heavy bloated I go to the gym to the iron machine I stand still and walk up stairs my face glistening with sweat I am aborting you.

I am eleven years old you are my baby you no longer need her breast she will not give it to you you have teeth you bite her she screams. My breasts are sore with your screams I am old twenty-five and a thousand my breasts are still sore with your screams. I hold you in my arms I comfort you you bite you are hungry ravenous insatiable.

Sweat trickles down my forehead my short hair wet my muscles aching I am purging you. The machine creaks underneath my weight the weight of words waiting. I push my arms shaking I count in my head the room loud with men grunting humid with the smell of sweat. Repetitions finished my reflection in the mirror body enormous tired aching wet.

I am eleven years old my body pretending to be strong I carry you my arms full you fill the room with your hunger. I am twelve years old I carry you sometimes I let you walk my body is weakening my resistance lessened the memories weighing me down the ground sinking beneath me I am heavy. I am twelve years old I look in the mirror I am enormous I do not eat I will be light I am no longer strong. You walk behind me follow in my footsteps I hide from you I will not show you my weakness my fear the scars deep purple on my body.

You lie next to me your small body in the darkness fine curls against your cheeks my body aching with the pain. I reach down and peel the scars off my legs make them invisible they are my scars for no one else to see. You see them you are little with big eyes you know my scars you hold them in your tiny hands you stroke them kiss them with wet lips. I watch you sleep my mind tortured I have transferred the scars no longer on my legs they are under my forehead below my breast.

You begin to speak my little one you want to name me who am I what is my name? I have no name. I watch you as you move through the world you want to name me you need to classify you long to create order you cannot order me. My body turns toward you you are not mine you are not my skin not my flesh I am not you you are not me. You cannot name me I watch you grow we are growing apart you search for my name among the rubble of our detachment. Soon you will resist me you will fight the body that gave you life that gave me life. Today you are still little two years old three years old learning to talk you have a voice it is strong it reverberates where are those shirts you scream those twenty shirts?

* * *

I walk through the rain it creates channels on my skin streams I build a dam it covers me runs along my scars washes me. People huddled in storefronts crowded umbrellas sagging clothes rumpled. The water leaves paths on my skin drawing me inventing me. The sky breaks on my head I watch the world open I am drowning this is my story.

Your twenty shirts are dry they won't see the sky as it falls they are safe from the catastrophes I invent they are safe from me. Your twenty shirts are clean and whole not ripped and fragmented they have not lived they are plastic bound on hangers sterile. I have no clean shirts no iron to smooth them out my hamper full and over-flowing clothes dirty with life and time. I am dirty my body marked smooth and strong imperfect and sagging no plastic wrap no money back no guarantee.

You lean toward me pick me up we are going to my place you say come with me. I am imperfect I say my footsteps unsure my words broken yes you say come with me. I watch you I wait for the fear. You are not scared. We leave the painting on my wall I leave my bed I begin with you I let myself approach you you are my lover I will walk beside you today. You take my hand I take your hand we look ahead our eyes focused on one-another we are together forever our forever today much longer than the twenty shirts that will remain unnoticed never dirty they do not live.

Today I am wet my body soaked warm rain still drip-ping into my eyes hair flat against my head. Soon you will come to me nineteen shirts on the back seat of your car one dirty waiting to be returned. They guarantee one day service fifteen percent off a cheap way to keep the sem-blance to stave off life. Your shirts will be clean forever never marked by life. You will come to me you will take off your shirt the one that belongs to that place that holds you eight hours every day the one they pay you to wear the one that guarantees a life of cleanliness no marks no impurities. You will come to me naked your body alive with the traces of time.

* * *

The Watch

You come to me with a watch hanging on a string. The watch is silver antique with initials carved Y B G your beautiful gaze you say. I tie it around my neck close to my heart I hear it ticking. It does not keep time.

You can return it you say it has a warranty. No I say. I hang it on my window sometimes I wear it around my neck I like to look at it sunlight rain reflected through the glass I set it to anytime I want it keeps my time.

I am caught in your time. Your time does not live in my world. I can't keep up with you your time always too short too long. The clock the watch the radio keep your time they say three o'clock soon. After three in your time it will be four always a difficult time for me my colic time maman says babies cry in the afternoon. I am not a baby I am twenty-five and a thousand. You say three o'clock almost four I must run home to my watch and change the time. My watch wound in my hand it is nine o'clock morning or night this watch keeps time twenty-four hours then it stops. Twenty-four hours is long enough.

You are my lover. You give me the magic watch for my birthday. It is not a birthday present you say it is a talisman like Covenant's ring. You read me the books the ones about Thomas Covenant about white gold and courage. This is your talisman you say, your white gold.

* * *

I am thirteen I do not have white gold no talisman I am trying to keep time that is not mine. My baby is growing you are four you are five curls to your shoulders. It is Saturday I go to the bakery the place where I work hot bread white whole wheat whole grain out of the oven date squares carrot cake dark rich brownies croissants I eat and eat and eat. Your time is not mine the days are long I cannot keep up afternoons evenings you are growing they are fighting I am tired. More bread hot soft burning my tongue butter honey chocolate blueberries ice cream I am eating the bakery I am the bakery come and eat me I am for sale. My stomach is full six o'clock the day over time to go home I am tired. Thirteen my body lean stomach flat breasts small hips narrow I stick my finger down my throat throw up undigested food into the toilet.

You are late for dinner maman says yes I am not hungry I say. I go to my room. My baby is growing you are not my baby anymore I am hungry black hole in my stomach I must eat. The walls in my room are shrinking my stomach is growing my ears listening for the sound of food I will clean up in the kitchen I say go to bed maman you are tired. Remnants of dinner quickly rice no butter vegetables cake just a sliver another one you won't notice peanut butter quick shhhh you can't hear me quick to the bathroom.

* * *

I meet you again my lover I have not known you long you don't know me I want to say. We lie next to each other on my small bed by the window I hide my head you can't see me I tell you. When did you start you ask I was thirteen I say I was working in a bakery.

* * *

At home no one notices they are busy caught in time I am invisible. The days are easier now I go to school to the library skip breakfast no lunch no dinner I come home I will clean up I say. Every night I clean up in the kitchen. You think I am helpful I am not I am selfish self-destructive disgusting. I am alone in my pain. There is no time for me.

* * *

How can I help you ask. We are lovers you say I would like to help you say. I am scared I say I am old twenty-five and a thousand I have been fighting this battle so long I have borrowed their time I am afraid to borrow yours. Fight this one with me you say hold my hand we will be together. You give me a watch that doesn't tell time. Now I have my own time.

Time has stopped my stomach full of food this terror will not disappear time is standing still. I am fourteen you are now four maman never there papa asleep head spinning I cannot move vomit everywhere.

* * *

Summer holidays I am fourteen I have my own room rented in a house they are friends of my parents. It is Wednesday today my day off I plan my binge. Bread and muffins first butter and honey green grapes nutella ice cream bars chocolate cookies my finger in my throat angry tears face blotchy. Again and again I throw up I eat and eat and eat my body is growing I am enormous. Outside they do not know they cannot see the traces of vomit on my face I open the bathroom door I am pretty sweet polite. The man in the house he knows I think I hate him he is a crazy man up all night light shining from his room downstairs. He comes into my room a pigsty he says this is shameful yes I think I am shameful go away.

I call you I am scared I have thrown up again it's Monday morning. Monday morning Tuesday afternoon Wednesday Thursday this is following me help me I am drowning in my vomit. You drive from work pick me up we are silent together lovers side by side you are brave you say. I am shameful I say enormous awful disgusting no you say you are beautiful. We drive to a café closeby I order a cappuccino large strong no sprinkles you drink hot chocolate it is cold outside we are buried under the world. Tears of rage I cry on your shoulder I am tired my body screaming ulcer bleeding.

I am fourteen I work all day I dance all night. I meet some guys they are older come with us they say we have cars you can stay at our place our parents are gone suburban houses open for the summer fertile for experimentation. How old are you they ask I do not tell them it is my secret. We dance together dance floor crowded bodies swaying drowsy with alcohol eyes floating expressions vacant drugged. I drink with you I don't like beer prefer cheap champagne I am classy you say come home with us you say I am tired I say giddy sick I have not eaten.

The man who owns the store screams at me I am tired you take me upstairs hands under my shirt I feel sick do not be late again you say. You leave the store I am alone hours crawl by. Six o'clock the sign says closed I count the money slide out the back door walk home slowly legs collapsing under the weight of my last binge my last defeat. Horns beeping tires screeching they stop their car in front of me I am too tired to walk too exhausted to refuse I see their silhouettes through my eyes half shut they drive me back to their place. Look at her you say she is beautiful take off her shirt. You like me I think you will not hurt me. Hands reaching for me I can't breathe bodies swelling mouths biting help I scream so quiet it is sleep I long for please put me to sleep.

* * *

When I am tired I set my watch to evening I pretend
night has fallen and I sleep. With my watch all time is my
own. When I am awake I set my watch back sometimes I
set it back every hour and there are fifty hours in my day.
Those are good days. Sometimes I set it forward and live
only for one hour. On those days you come to me my lover
we are together you read to me I tell you stories. Did I tell
you that story I ask? Your eyes cloud over with tears yes
you say you told me but it might have been another one
are there many left? I don't know, I say. I don't know.

* * *

Today I wear my watch around my neck. I am carrying
time. The time is twelve o'clock that time of forever that
is always in the middle. Today I do not want to remember
no memories I am exhausted every day another memory.
Just time around my neck today while I wait for tomorrow to come.

* * *

Blood

Blood rushes out of me. I have been waiting for it. Stomach muscles tight with cramps I want to scream blood bright red and black. Tiny I curl into a ball pain clutching your back still asleep. I have been waiting for this blood red cleansing I want to tell you I want to wake you from your sleep.

You are with me my lover for my first blood crimson pouring out of me onto white sheet staining your futon. It is my first blood I am twenty-four older than most pain has scared away my blood. You know more about blood than I do have held women while they curled into balls small on the large bed it is my first time. Today I am twenty-five and a thousand. Today I bleed again.

I am fourteen end of the summer I don't bleed I wonder if the blood is clogged inside me. I am not pregnant we have created nothing you forced yourself on my body there will be no child I will not eat.

I have not known you long my lover and I bleed. I will not create for you we create ourselves I am writing you into my book making you up as I go along. With you I bleed I wash the pain away. We lie together my hand holding my blood I laugh out loud. I love to see you laugh you say there is often sadness in your eyes.

Come with me I take your hand walk out with you the morning is waking up. Look at the sky I say red and yellow reflected on white snow still thin on the ground look the sky is bleeding my pain. You fill the white porcelain bath ankles in the snow hose spraying me as I stand beside you shivering I smear my blood on your body laughing. We lie together bodies immersed in the hot water stopping the flow of my blood and I tell you a story.

It is a story I wrote long ago I painted pictures to go with it I don't have it anymore it was stolen by a professor I lent it to him to read it he disappeared. Your gaze upon me blue eyes waiting I begin.

* * *

Once upon a time there was a boy. His name was Graham. Every day he went out to play with his pail and shovel on the yellow sand in front of the purple sea. The sea was beautiful dark and rich. For hours each day he sat and watched the purple waves glimmering green and blue and the magical birds flying above him. The sand castles grew big and majestic sometimes so big the giant spotted birds came flying down and sat on the turrets.

Every evening as the sun went down Graham walked home pail and shovel in hand through the grey bedraggled neighborhood where he lived. Every night as he opened the front door he heard his father screaming at his mother. "There is no money!" "Can't you come home earlier?" "You have a son, you know!" And every night he ran to his room hands held tightly over his ears.

One night Graham woke to hear his parents talking in hushed voices. "He's strange," he heard his father say, "he doesn't have any friends." "He goes off all day," said his mother, "God knows where." "Time to do something with the boy," replied his father, "make him into a man." "Can't have a wimp good-for-nothing for a son."

The next morning Graham woke feeling heavy. He looked around and saw that his room had been transformed. The walls that used to be painted gold with purple stars were grey. Where the paint was peeling there was old wallpaper showing. The curtains were no longer billowing in the wind the sweet sea smell entering his room. There were no curtains. There was no smell.

Quickly, Graham gathered his pail and shovel and ran outdoors past the torn-down buildings, under the clotheslines, through old work shirts, yellowed underwear, pink polyester blouses, his feet pounding on the gravel. Graham ran and ran, sure he was in a maze or running in a circle – where was the sea? Tired after a long day of searching, Graham walked home his feet leaden his body slumped forward.

"Where have you been?" asked his mother. Graham was too tired to answer. He walked into his room and closed the door behind him.

Day after day, Graham set out to find the purple sea with the words of his parents still fresh in his mind. He looked so hard that his eyes tired and when he returned home all colours had disappeared and everything was grey. At night he no longer dreamed and he was tired upon waking. After a few months, Graham stopped getting up in the morning. He gave up on ever finding the purple sea or seeing his friends on the beach again. All day, he lay in bed, his mind blank and grey.

One morning, many months later, he heard a knock n the door. Lazily, Graham walked to the door and opened it. In front of him he saw a young boy with a pail and shovel in his hand. "Hello Graham," the blond boy said with a twinkle in his eye, "where have you been?" "What are you talking about?" Graham asked, his voice full of disdain. "I am Jens," the boy said, "don't you remember me? We used to play together in front of the purple sea." "No," said Graham, "I don't remember," and he shut the door on the boy's face. But the boy was big and strong and he held the door open with his nose. "Please come back," he said to Graham," we miss you. I know you haven't forgotten us. You have just closed your eyes." And he left.

Graham walked slowly back into his room and lay down on his bed where he fell into a deep, colourful sleep. In his dreams he was on another planet and he lived in a castle. The planet had wings and flew high above the ground. From the gold castle, Graham spent his days counting the green sheep with the purple polka-dots and the silver snakes. He had dinner with magenta snails and tea with Ms. Lumpyheart-the-cloud. Sometimes his planet was a bouncing ball that leaped on and off the earth and once in a while it shrunk and he could take it home with him and hide it under his bed.

Graham woke with a start the next morning. When he opened his eyes, he was blinded by a ray of purple sunlight. Could it be? he thought to himself. He inhaled. Deep into his lungs he could feel the sea air. Graham leapt out of bed and throwing on his clothes with his right hand, he picked up his pail and shovel and ran toward the smell that was filling his body, making him so light that he could fly! Graham ran and ran he didn't stop until the waves covered his body and he could feel the fuchsia fish leaping onto him. He turned around and saw all of his old friends gathered around him. "Nice to have you back," they said. "Welcome home."

* * *

You climb out of the bathtub fingers wrinkled you hand me the white towel. Our hot feet melting the snow we run back to the house we huddle under the warm covers of your bed. What happened to your story, you ask, where did he go with it? I don't know. He stole my words my drawing he left I never saw him again. Today I find them the words are still there imprinted on my body. Today I lend them to you.

* * *

Night has fallen I am not sleeping the blood keeps me awake I am waiting to turn into a monster. I have seen the purple sea I have seen the silver snakes listened to the gossiping clouds I am waiting for your visit I will terrify you I am medusa. One look at me and you will turn to stone I will smear my blood over your body paint you red.

I am alone pacing into the night a creature of darkness give me your words I will consume them digest them excrete them. I do not want your words I have my own. I am a monster you have created me I am dripping with blood it is your blood flowing out of my body you are drowning in my blood.

I have told you a story I have given you my blood my body. You listen to my body you build sandcastles on my spine swim in my purple sea sleep nestled in my short red hair you are my body.

The Screen

Every morning I switch on my screen. You appear before me. I have read your name a hundred times have read your words you exist for me I know you. It is 1993 and the Net is my tie to the world. With you I communicate it is safe I can logout save delete anytime all day all night.

One hundred messages this morning on the screen do I want to read? delete? logout? My finger rests on the return button eyes accustomed to scanning I look for your words the ones that touch my heart. Your name does not appear this morning I cannot find you you are not a Sender today you are a Subject. I read words written about you. They say that you are dead. How can you die? Words cannot die.

One hundred messages this morning one hundred messages about you. Your death reaches me reaches all of us continents apart we feel the silence of the Net missing your words. I want to touch you my body is disappearing what is this medium that allows us to be so close with only words and names to identify us?

I print out the comments my printer grudgingly spewing your death. I want to keep you alive I will not stop writing I will hold on to you trace your outline on my body recreate you reach for you behind this screen.

I read a piece you wrote the night of your death a piece about bodies-without-organs you who dies so suddenly body ravaged by diabetes. You write about the concern that our being-in-the-world will be replaced by being-in/being-with/being-one-with the machine... I need the machine I need it to reach to you to heal my broken body I need your words on my screen every morning I write with you. Your words are imprinted on my mind dancing behind my eyes you are reading, deleting, saving, replying, harvesting. We need to speak. The Net is our medium our body-without-organs.

I wonder about the irony of discussing embodiment by e-mail I wonder what you look like did you suffer? We must not abandon the body.

Your words. "At the limits of the body, speech is abandoned, death sinks in, the Net is hidden speech. And at the limits, cries and murmurs are heard. Broken, disconnected, this is all we have to offer."

* * *

I see you behind my screen I see the reflection of myself. Today I wear the watch my talisman around my neck and keep time that is my own. Your presence gone leaves a crease in my heart. I do not have an iron I cannot iron it out smooth the pain. I hear the ticking of my watch. Time is passing.

You appear and disappear on my screen. I have saved many pieces of you I can print out your body your words alive in front of me months of yours are mine I have saved them copied them rewritten them.

My floor is dirty spotted with paint it will not come off it is the witness of my creation this morning I paint for you these colours the curve of the paintbrush the agility of my fingers on the keys this is for you for me.

* * *

Psychoanalysis

I am looking for an analyst they tell me analysis might be my cure it might suture my brain make my mind whole recreate me in a way that might allow me to live with myself. I begin my search carrying my life in a little pack on my back the apostrophes the commas the colons the semi-colons tied to my feet question marks in my ears.

You are the first one I meet I have left my voice on their machines I wait for their calls. I know nothing about analysis I have lent out my mind before it didn't help I am scared. I am late you summon me directly into your office the room in which you will analyse me. The walls close in on me high ceiling dark furniture you have modeled your office after your title. This is *the analyst* the office says you are the patient. The office must be cold impersonal unassuming yet daunting with dusty books Freud on the covers papers covering the desk notebook on your lap. Lie down you say the couch is blue polyester you sit behind me your feet up you listen.

This office is different. I am facing you you are sitting in a black leather chair I can almost touch you. You are rich I am going to make you richer room in good taste large so posh. Elephants burgundy Persian rugs black leather couch large windows I feel safe here you will take care of me you are successful. Over your moustache you look at me I don't like your moustache your eyes are small how did you become so rich? "You will pay me directly," you say. Yes, I think. I am your decorator.

I am late. Why do you think you are late you ask. Because I didn't leave myself enough time to get here I think but that will not do you will have to analyse it this will add to your reputation you will exist through me I will send you new patients you will include me in your case study.

Your office understated warm beige carpet beige painting on the wall beige couch. I cannot analyse you you say you need more than I have to offer you say. You were late you say you are not ready for me.

You talk about the light at the end of the tunnel about taking care of the child within about love and peace and shame. You sit in front of me I am interviewing you with my life you are my fourth analyst this is me dissect me show me your talents help me give you something to fix tell me if I can be helped. From across the room I look at you your face friendly expectant you can see me every Sunday too. Can you see me? Paintings made by your children on the walls stick men tractors bees scribbles you look at them with pride clutching your cup of tea. Why are you here you ask, tell me about yourself. I come to you fragmented have left my arms in Freud's office my feet with the rich man my eyes in the beige room. I can help you we can help each other you say we must communicate with the child within come back tomorrow.

For a week I play analyst-hopping. Eleven o'clock with Freud twelve-fifteen the child-within two o'clock how much will this session cost. Five o'clock I am dead have written too many stories words unspoken have warmed your chair have paid for your new carpet your new painting your tea.

The child-within is boring me I long to leave the hour is too long. I must go I tell you I am tired I do not tell you I will not return. In the rich man's office I talk about my analyst-hopping I am ashamed. I cannot help you the rich man tells me you need analysis five times a week I cannot give you that much time you must go elsewhere.

In the streets I feel alone. One more analyst my game is almost over what if you won't have me I will be alone again what if I can't be helped I will be crazy forever.

I will see you every day Freud tells me you will come in the mornings lie on the couch tell me about your dreams pay me in advance. I try not to notice that you are falling asleep I need you I want you to exorcise my soul (these are your words) I want to be cleaned out pink with sparkles not this deep magenta that hurts when I bend the wrong way. I tell you my dreams I dream for you to write them down. I am scared on your couch I cannot see your face what are you looking at you eat an apple I can hear your knife cut it into quarters it crunches between your teeth you slurp your juice chew gum bite into a candy fall asleep. I throw up the sound of your slurp haunts my sleep I eat and eat and eat.

I return to you every day cry when I leave you open me up do not sew me back together we are finished for today you say you do not say goodbye. I leave walk into the store fill the gaps you have opened stick them together with cinnamon buns date squares butter tarts I throw up. I return to you I have nowhere else to go. Every day I have less to say I hear you snoring I can't bear the slicing the slurping the chewing I think of the combinations of food I will use to stop the pain I long to turn around to scream WAKE UP. I am quiet well-mannered I was taught to keep my mouth shut don't interrupt. What are you thinking you always ask are you afraid you missed my words you were asleep again. One day I tell you I am uncomfortable perhaps afraid you might fall asleep what does it bring up you ask this has nothing to do with me you say it's your father your mother your fear you say slurping and chewing. I am quiet I have no words. You do not exist you tell me you are created through other people you cannot bear for them to fall asleep because you only exist through their gaze. You are not looking at me you do not acknowl-edge me you fall asleep I do not exist.

The streets are cold heat rising from the snow bright blue sky I am alone I am not here this is not me please tell me who I am. I cannot dream I do not sleep my waking hours bland I am numb.

Today you tell me you cannot help me if I won't speak I try to open my mouth nothing emerges I have no words you will fall asleep you kill me with your sleep. It is eleven o'clock I look at my watch what are you thinking you ask I don't know I say when will this end one by one the sec-onds pass my watch has stopped. I sleep when I am awake I am not alive I walk through the streets throw up undi-gested food you tell me I am a monster a parasite I feel like a mosquito I suck your blood you squish me between your thumb and index finger.

I meet another analyst your office small unassuming you ask me about myself I tell you he falls asleep you are angry. Leave him you say he is sucking your spirit out of your body you say you do exist you say I will help you you say. My sixth analyst. I am scared I feel like a bouncing ball in one office out the other more food for your stories while I disappear. The next one is gentle you can't stay with me you say you are too complex I will help you I will find someone for you I know where to look. I am tired I let you do the work come to see you once a week tell you bits about myself conceal others I am tired.

Now I have found you. My lucky analyst-number-sev-en. You do not promise a cure I can stay crazy this is me I am relieved. Before you accept me into your world you send me to one more analyst this time for an assessment you want to know if this is the right treatment I go to him.

Another office grey carpets this time I feel comforta-ble. Your face is soft you look at me when I talk you listen. I am nervous I want to hear you say that this will be my cure that I will grow into myself through analysis I want to know that I have been fighting the right battle giving my body to a worthwhile cause. I tell you about myself soon I am talking freely I have found my language I can speak I laugh you laugh with me. The session is over one hundred and fifteen dollars to ask you for your opinion will I do well am I a candidate? Yes. You need a language you say you will create yourself through analysis you will learn to speak the pain you will make it part of you part of your experience you will write the story yes you do exist you say he was wrong you will soar you can fly good luck and courage you say. I am already flying you believe in me I am happy yes I will fly look at me I am flying!

Today I sit in your office purple walls orange chairs a couch in that other room a little further away. I do not yet lie on the couch you are preparing me first I must trust you you listen when I speak look into my eyes when I am quiet. Today I know I am alright we will not change me I am relieved I will not be cured I will come every day. We will work together I will tell you stories my fiction my truth you will piece the stories together sometimes I will dream you will record my dreams and we will analyse them together.

* * *

This morning we sit in a café jazz playing softly people walking in and out. Take out your map. We are going on a journey. Look carefully bring it closer to your eyes put on your reading glasses. On the right hand corner trace the thick red line with your index finger. Put the map down set it on the table keep your finger on the red line. Hold your finger. Stop moving. Where the red line stops look closely. Move your face down nose almost touching the red line look closely do you see the tiny purple veins can you see the faint traces of life look very closely move your finger take off your glasses. Follow those traces with your eyes surround yourself with the lines tie them onto your body dive into the map. You are the map. Now follow me.

You will need a microscope today we will follow that thin purple line which begins at the corner of your left eye. Feel the line with your finger explore the contours caress the bumps. This is our journey.

* * *

I am fifteen years old I do not live here anymore my life is in my dreams I cannot see you I do not exist. I dream of another place a time when I feel no pain a time when I do not stuff myself with food a time when I do not hear you cry softly in your room. Sometimes you come home you are not my mother you are my child I hold you in my arms take care of you whisper in your ear. You are scared life is growing outside you feel the streets alive with people you come home to die. I know you must leave I am selfish I want to feel you here but you are not really here you have no home. Your child grows without you she is strong the cord severed she is neither mine nor yours. Sometimes I long to confide in you to tell you about the food that rots inside me the food I swallow without tasting the food that tries to fill the gaps. You have no ears you have left them with the books waiting for you on the desk by the window on the third floor of the library. You dream of returning to your books.

When you can't leave when you must stay home you pile your books on the kitchen table the kitchen is out of bounds. You hold the key to my hunger my stomach screams for food it will not be appeased you are locked in for hours you sleep your head on the table I dare not enter it is your domain my stomach belongs to you. You do not eat the books are your food I am jealous my stomach demanding growing I am enormous I throw up your body perfect thin lithe never hungry mine ravenous. The two of you do not speak anymore you do not see him he does not exist. I hold him from you you can not breathe he swallows your air I am your bodyguard I am your body.

He does not speak he fills his lungs and goes to sleep the lights are turned down we must not wake him. Sometimes he wakes he moves your books he is angry they are invading the house his life is piled up with your books you speak for him now he is silent you are reading away his voice he is disappearing up down bipolar he is scared he screams at you you cry you long for your desk at the library where your books are waiting.

I am fifteen I dream of another place. Soon I will leave I am old have already lived too long. She has grown up her curls reach her shoulders she wakes at night her screams leave cracks in the freshly painted walls. You scold her these walls must not be cracked you say the house must be kept clean and beautiful don't drop the bowl don't make a mess don't eat in front of the television don't walk on the carpet don't enter the living room don't leave crumbs no dirty dishes don't breathe too loud. She does not listen she screams at night breaks your favourite bowl watches television all of the time cereal on her knees. I am quiet never disturb you I throw up quietly while my brother sleeps he does not wake he waits until the house is dark and then he moves like a cat strumming his guitar.

One day you enter my closet find ten pails of vomit. I have to wait for you to go to sleep then I flush them down the toilet during the day I throw up in my room. You find the vomit you question me. I feel sick sometimes I tell you. You are too tired to push me you say no more you tell me I must stop. Yes I say I am relieved I go back to my room I throw up.

No one must know I must be careful not to let them see me I snap on my happy face put make up around the dark circles of my eyes I leave the house and go to school. At school I do not hear them I dream of my escape I write stories in my head I take out my map and trace my journey.

* * *

Total Recall

Tonight I watch a movie. You watch me watch. On the screen the men pull out their guns shoot one another you don't flinch I feel nausea I close my eyes. It is a movie about total recall.

In the movie the man searches for memory. Your actions are more important than your memories the wise one tells him. I am enthralled with the plot sickened by the violence. It is my life.

His memories are my memories they flood my mind. Like him I don't know. Are these memories real? They invade my mind they create me make me take a step forward try to justify my pain my existence.

I look for the parallels. He is a fictitious character I am a fictitious character. He is persecuted by memories that invade his sleep memories he does not understand memories that have a deep effect on his waking hours. He buys a dream vacation from a company that will implant new memories new fictions into his mind memories that will allow him to live his fantasy to be who he has always dreamed of being. I go to analysis. He begins to remember takes charge of his life takes action. I write a book.

The movie upsets me I cannot take my eyes off the screen this is not my type of movie this is not the life I am living this is not me. There is no accountability the men kill and kill and kill they don't look back why did you rape me where are you the one who screamed at me why didn't you say sorry when you hit me do you remember?

* * *

I am fifteen far away from home I have escaped. The landscape has changed the language is different I want to understand I hold my ear to the ground hear the heartbeat of this new place adjust my heart. The new language seeps into my body turns into air that fills my lungs. I have found a new voice I speak another language I meet you.

I remember nothing I have flown away I have no past no age no name I am who you make me I exist within the new words I learn each day your hand on my skin your touch inventing me. I meet you I do not fall in love I feel close to you you remind me of my father. Soon you engulf me want me to be yours want to possess my words I am weak have come without nails to tie my feet to the ground I need you to hold me down.

You take me in put new words into my mouth we live together sleep together eat together laugh together fight together we are each other. You want to speak my language the one I left at home I want to speak yours we are speaking machines we speak so many languages we have stopped listening.

I am fifteen I am living with you we are married by words we do not understand. Night after night I wake cold sweat covers my body I dream of words I left at home I dream of a time that no longer exists I can't tell you my dreams I have forgotten those words I do not write them down you comfort me with empty words.

My new life means a new me I repeat to myself I want to be different I will not recall there will be no memories I deny myself the threads that hold me together. When you approach me want to touch my body demand closeness I push you away I will not share my past with you I will not let you touch my body black and blue.

In my mind I rehearse my new language I learn only the words I choose to include into my vocabulary. I teach you my language we communicate within the limits of the trapeze I walk along that leads nowhere. I long to desire you to feel my heart the way you tell me yours grows swells tingles when I approach you. My heart is made of stone. I do not find a word for desire.

* * *

A few years pass. I leave you behind. I am wandering my heart in my hand I don't know where to place it I am searching for lost memories I don't know where to look. I sit in front of the cafeteria my body unmoving the halls buzzing university students everywhere. I try to sew my heart into my leg there I won't see it won't feel it. It does not fit. I dig a hole so big I can hide inside I do not walk my legs will not support me I cannot escape. I sit against the cold iron rail it leaves a red mark on my back you approach me hold out your hand. I have seen you before orange eyes snakes for hair I do not turn to stone I watch you transfixed.

Entwined we walk arm in arm almost the same height you spell out the words I insert them letter by letter with a silver spoon into my heart. Carefully you wash my chest above my breasts bruised by my pounding fists bruised by the words I cannot speak the breasts I long to slice off blood rushing down you brush your lips against mine leaving a faint orange smell you insert my heart leave no scar. You lie next to me our bodies very close not quite touching you caress my face don't say a word I do not pull away.

Christmas comes you know I am alone. We make a plan to go out to dinner I have always wanted to be served course after course to delight in the miniscule works of art served to warm my soul and gently fill my stomach. With you I think I can eat.

The food arrives in colours. Yellow first a colour that will pave the way with gold. The second plate a touch of orange the background red. I don't look at the food I look into your eyes swallow the colour feel my breath quicken my skin soften. Desire overflowing you take my hand I swallow you whole I eat. Traces of magenta spots of peacock blue I am a stream touch me wash yourself my water is clean pure fresh. The main course burgundy your eyes alight I have no words my heart is open I cannot speak devour me taste me savour me. We linger over dessert our hands now by our sides we have not spoken we have uttered no words we understand each other. Merry Christmas you say, would you like to spend the night?

The night is cold it is the middle of winter I walk home I do not spend the night with you. This last night I will savour alone I love you we will be together always I will speak again you will help me heal the invisible scars where you inserted my heart. The next morning you are gone. I never see you again.

You sewed me up too soon. My heart still aches.

* * *

Last night I watched a movie a violent movie about memory and I remembered you a painful memory. I remembered the way the ground lifted when your feet glided over it I remembered the way you smoked half your cigarette and then lost interest I remembered the way you made me feel I remembered the colours I remembered the touch we never shared I missed you my memory violent.

Last night I watched a movie a violent movie about memory and I remembered you a violent memory. I remembered the way you closed me in the way you hit me when I tried to get away the way you forced me down the way you used your weight I remembered your sorrow your apologies I remembered the red roses the promises the pain the violence my memory violent.

Last night I watched a movie and I remembered.

* * *

I am sitting in the womb that is the memory that we create together. Analysis long today I tell you that I am big enormous I want to throw up. Every word I write makes me grow I am reaching to the moon I can touch it with my index finger the world is my memory.

Still face to face you repeat my words make sense of them create a space for me to enter into. The room takes on my shape my body creating contours smoothing out the corners raising the ceiling. I feel your gaze upon me I look away play with the hem of my dress I long to reach out to you to feel your body as it holds the memory of me.

* * *

The words stick firmly to my fingers today they will not flow I cannot release them I am afraid to let them go. Each letter creates a boundary between me and the callus that is my body. I am hardening. Soon you will no longer penetrate me.

At night I dream of you. I lie on the bed my body still not responding to yours I feel the scratching of your fingers as you reach for the opening of my heart. You scratch at the surface you think you will soon cut the skin but you are not touching me you are pulling apart the letters that create the words that create me. It is my story you uncover. You scream at me fingernails clawing. Frenetically you reach for me the letters jumping at you peeling out your eyes piercing your chest pulling your hair. What have you done what is this you scream enraged as you unravel the words the sentences the commas the periods the colons of my body where are you? I am here I say quietly this is my body. Read it.

My body is no longer the site for your anger no longer the playground for your destruction. My body is the parchment on which I piece the letters together. My body is my story.

The cappuccino leaves a bitter taste in my mouth I am remembering I am unpeeling the layers. I am the onion maman spelled out on the phone o-n-i-o-n the one you thought I could not understand. I am the onion the one that appeared unsolicited in all my food the one I swallowed unwillingly. I have eaten myself I have thrown myself up. Today I swallow myself whole I keep myself intact.

* * *

I am fifteen I am sixteen I am seventeen the years blend in my mind. I move through the world parts of my body separate I leave them behind I am fragmented you cannot touch all of me there is no whole. I have stopped fighting I am passive I cannot feel your touch I throw you up afterwards. Sadness leaves rashes on my soul that will not go away.

Today I remember. A wave of sadness rushes over me I cannot return to the past a festering mass in my joints rotting my bones. Events swim with the dying fish as they near the shore I cannot tell them apart the water is murky polluted. On the beach I see a red sign do not swim it says these waters are contaminated I am in the water up to my waist the tide is coming in soon I will be covered.

The muscles in my face are tense I am scared the sea of memories pushing me further and further from the shore. There are no lifeguards. I imagine myself as Edna Pontellier swimming out further and further into the sea never to return.

I am alone today. The man sitting to my left cannot see me he is looking into his cup of coffee afraid to look up afraid he will see himself. I have not swum out to sea I have stayed in my chair like the character in the movie who pays for his fantasy and lives it implanted in his brain as he sits quietly in his chair. Total Recall.

* * *

My stomach full I sit my words forming themselves on the screen. I have swallowed myself whole have eaten the pain the anguish the terror the desperation. My mouth is wired shut I have no words to express this bloated feeling. You have invaded me entered me soon I will explode. The music is loud to my ears it is crawling inside me the filters of my soul breaking my story no longer my own. I can feel you inside me your toes pushing against my abdomen your fingers reaching for my breasts head caught in my throat I can't breathe. You are big a grown-up man an invader you have corrupted me have implanted a new memory inside my body. I am purging you today.

The café reappears around me. Soon I will tell you a story I will move from this pain that is consuming me I will have thrown you up your nails no longer scratching at my heart. Beside me I see you look at me I see the traces of a smile on your lips two women deep in conversation they don't notice you looking. Two young boys enter one wears an earing in his left ear they stand next to one-another. Around them the café shrinks their presence stronger than their surroundings.

* * *

I think I have known you forever. You have always been my lover. You are strong your lean muscles pressing against my memories you help me set fire to them you squeeze the life out of them you blow them away.

We do not speak of what we have weary of names and labels we do not order do not classify do not plan. In a forgotten cupboard you find your wedding ring misplaced it is no longer on your finger you are free we meet each other in the middle of your freedom. For a month we spend most days together I tell you stories we write them on the sheets lay them beneath the pillows dream them re-invent them in the mornings. The days fly by sometimes we don't get out of bed it is our home the place where our bodies meet the place we hide the words left unspoken.

A million meters of snow have closed us in we do not venture out into the world. I weave myself into your body. You draw patterns on my stomach between my hip bones and my ribs you watch my skin tighten in anticipation you feel my body beckoning you reaching out for you quivering with desire.

One night you tell me not to count on you.

You are my lover.

One night you tell me not to count on you not to count on you not to count on you. Goose bumps on my skin my body freezes I am dead. You tell me that you will perhaps soon leave. You tell me you must not lose your own life. I hear you. You think I am devouring you I am swallowing you whole. That night I die.

* * *

A woman interrupts my memory asks me what I am writing you I say here you are in the middle of my story. She says no tell me what do you write about you don't know me how can you write me into your story? I don't show it to her. This is my body. It is only for me to see and for you and you and you.

* * *

That night I don't feel your body as it reaches out for mine. I don't feel your fingers clasping onto mine I don't hear the tears you long to cry I do not know you. Your words reverberate in my mind I am in a cathedral can you hear them echo my head is exploding. My sleep disturbed I plan to leave in the morning I will shovel my way through the million meters of snow that surround us I will crawl through the terrible cold that envelops us. My escape forms in my mind our dreams are separate you sleep with your eyes open you look at me silent. Dawn breaks I sharpen my fingers and begin to dig my way out of your soul. You do not scream you do not say a word my fingers draw blood you are silent. I dig and dig and dig my tears melting the snow turning it to ice the path more and more treacherous I hear the avalanches in the distance.

Come back. Stay with me. Hold me. The avalanches are dangerous. Don't risk your life.

I feel your hand reach out to mine you pull me back you do not say a word I am alone in my thoughts I have erected a barrier it reaches to the moon. Your hold on me is strong I want to let myself fall into your arms don't play with me I say I do not like to play games. I am not playing you say.

* * *

A woman walks by she is so thin I can see the bird flying out of her neck. She is another memory. I feel her hand on my body the imprint of her face superimposed onto mine we are the same I have been you you are me. She walks past me her head held high she remembers me I am her future. Her legs stiff with hunger she drops herself into a chair. Her hands like skeletons she wraps herself around the water she will sip for hours. I have been her. She is my past she is my future. She doesn't look at me she pretends she is invisible she thinks I do not see her she thinks I do not know. I have been you I think and soon you will be me. You are written on my body.

* * *

The Wanderer

*Now as Zarathustra was climbing the mountain he thought of
how often since his youth he had wandered alone and how many
mountains and ridges and peaks he had already climbed.*

*I am a wanderer and a mountain climber, he said to his heart;
I do not like plains, and it seems I cannot sit still for long. And
whatever may yet come to me as destiny and experience will include some wandering and mountain climbing: in the end one
experiences only oneself.*

I am moving with the pain. Every day I imagine another
place where I might find myself another home. I move
without direction I don't pack my bags anymore I have
enough to carry around inside. I am seventeen I am sixteen I am fifteen.

I move into your house I have been here three months
I am fading there are no colours. I look around everything
colourless an ikea house colourless couch colourless carpets matching colourless paintings I cannot find myself.

We move into our own place hungry for colour I buy a
red carpet paint the curtains yellow orange purple. Soon
my world is coming apart once more the bathroom is my
home I am treading in a swamp of vomit the colours fading in the sun as I try to block out the world.

I am fifteen I am sixteen I am seventeen I have already
lived a thousand years my skin is wearing thin my secrets

are eating at my bones I am crumbling. I move with the wind sometimes north sometimes west I drift with only the book I write in and the black clothes I wear each day. This time I go to Spain.

The ride is long you read my sign and pick me up you are going to the border will take me there eight hours closer to my goal. I do not dream of Spain I do not dream of anything my limbs are tired I am running from myself I am looking for colours that do not fade. You are older you ask where I am going tell me it is dangerous to go alone. I am not alone I tell you I am old old old two and a thousand I am here with you you smile I feel safe with you you are gentle you do not reach out to touch me do not capture me with your eyes. Let me drive by my home you say and I will take you to Luxemburg we will go out to dinner I will take you swimming in a lake. We eat together swim together you do not touch me do not walk on the freshly laid carpet I have placed at my feet I am safe with you my carpet is still clean unmarked no dirt no stains. Take a train you tell me not everyone is like me you plead. Yes I say. I do not take the train. I look for danger in my wanderings now I am big big bigger than two I look for someone to tell me where I am going I look for you.

Through France I do not see the landscape I cross the border into Spain I am seventeen I have been around the world alone have seen too much I see nothing. I walk I hitchhike I take the train awake asleep I eat throw up. Trains melt into trains rooms into rooms I am in a dream a nightmare from which I do not wake I have no money I wander aimlessly through the streets pretending I have somewhere to go. On the beach I sleep when the sun comes up pretend to brown my skin fall into a wordless slumber. You lie next to me rub your body against mine. I don't wake up at first I think it is a nightmare. And then I open my eyes you are there speaking in a language foreign I am too tired to understand you your hands digging into me body rubbing you cannot find me I am not beneath your touch. Frantic your fingers reach for the seam of my bathing suit faded yellow you reach for my nipple do not reach down to feel the scar you are burning into my skin. I have no words I do not respond to your probing fingers you are not touching me. You slap my face fucking Americans you say people begin to arrive you get up to leave I have failed you have not acknowledged your manliness have not aroused you I am a failure I go back to sleep.

I am seventeen I have travelled a million miles have seen your face before have felt your touch against my skin have smelled your acrid breath have died under the weight of your body I am alone.

The country moves with me the trains the streets the cars the beaches my home I wander. Nights become days. Tourist season has not arrived the beaches deserted I build my bedroom among the grains of sand I dig myself a grave to house the body I leave behind one word at a time. I begin to understand their language it is my fourth tongue I have left many words behind. The wind blows I do not feel the strong sun clawing at my body while my thoughts fade to grey. In the morning my skin bright red bumps forming body swollen from the sun I cannot move. I prepare for my death my skin fermenting fever rising I am delirious. They find me.

I wake up in a mansion I think I am in Greece they tell me I have a fever they feed me water and orange juice sometimes. The walls are high whitewashed with echoing halls I long to speak have only ghosts for company. The days melt one into one another my skin healing slowly the sun has ravaged me. I must dig up my grave withdraw my words before they find them they do not listen won't let me go they say I am sick I must stay in bed I am not sick I want to say I have no words I left them on the beach buried in the sand my body craves what I cannot say I must uncover them. Twelve o'clock the nurse enters feeds me my pills asks why I stayed alone on the beach tells me I could have died I am dead can't you see I tell her my words are gone I have left my body behind.

They fix my body wrap me with wet towels feed me oranges I ask them for more I need colour I tell them. The country blooms as I recover the trees bright red white yellow. I recover with the colours.

Today I walk outside they cover me straw hat on my head soft cotton clothes to mute the marks of my death the holes through which I allowed my spirit to escape. The beach is different my home erased flooded by the tourists bodies roasting in the sun children building castles on my grave. In the air I feel my spirit it is playing with the children it is the light in the turrets of their castles it is the food the lovers feed one-another it is sleep as it descends upon the parents tired of keeping watch. I pick my spirit up a little at a time I can only carry a little bit I am weak still. I leave the rest with them.

In Madrid the train stops and I call them the connection unclear I tell them about my bulimia come home they say we will climb together. I take the next plane. I am two and a thousand. I am a wanderer.

* * *

One must learn to look away from oneself in order to see much: this hardness is necessary to every climber of the mountains.

My plane lands I have come around the world my papa waits for me my eyes clouded with tears I have told you my secret the one that grows each day enveloping me sucking my blood killing me. You are cool with me quiet you drive me home. Maman sits in the chair by the wood stove a book in your hand your eyes closed you are sleeping. An old language emerges from my lips we talk all night you are gentle tonight you listen to me maybe you want to know my secret? You do not ask. We should sleep you say the morning rising out of the horizon I know you will not go to bed you sleep your head buried in your books they are your home your bed your life. For me you look up from your books keeps your eyes half open you almost see me.

I am seventeen well-behaved I will not speak of my secret again it makes you uncomfortable I will allow you to be my saviour. You see only yourself you cannot see me your eyes are closed to my pain it is your pain you see. I swallow my food do not throw up for three weeks you think I am saved we do not mention the fact that children are starving in Ethiopia we do not say that I am weak we do not question the perfection we have created we do not touch the strings that connect us. They are rotting. We are a family we stick together we do not speak our pain.

I am a wanderer it is time to leave I have allowed you to touch me I have spoken your words nodded at your commands listened to your suggestions you have not cured me my pain has not subsided I am leaving. We kiss goodbye you look triumphant I carry your confidence in my travel-bag set it beside the new clothes you bought me beside the love you showed me. I am alone.

* * *

Today I write from another chair looking out another window I am a wanderer I wander from one memory to another on the runways of my life.

* * *

I land in another city. In this city I have already written my initials in bathroom stalls my name is written on the wall. I unpack your confidence rent a room in a house with a couple. Their house is white he an architect she a psychologist they take me in help me transform the confidence into lingerie I wear next to my skin. They admire me look at me do not see me my body ravaged. I have a room it is my own I have a travel-bag full of new clothes I have lace lingerie laced with confidence I have two lovers making love we share a wall. I wear the lingerie next to my skin you brush my hair powder my face smooth the quills of the secret I have buried. I have told my secret once I do not tell it again I tie my hands behind my back keep them far from my mouth far from my throat I heal the callus that has formed on my hand the one made by my teeth.

At night I sleep soundly I hear her breathing through the wall feel his arm gently caressing her. The shutters against my window stay closed.

* * *

Last night I forgot to close the shutters you came in with the darkness you are the night you are invading me help! I am naked hot under my covers my lingerie discarded on the dresser. You break the glass that I forgot to seal enter me cut my lingerie into shreds the lace bleeds you escape with the wind.

Morning comes the sun does not shine through my window. We call the superintendent look we say there is no sun what can be done? The superintendent promises says he will send an expert we wait for days and weeks no one comes to see the darkness it is invading me I cannot live without sunlight I am suffocating.

Three months have passed I am a wanderer it is time to leave we shut the door of my room we draw a picture it is black do not enter it says the words invisible in the darkness. A few years later I hear you had to leave as well we didn't stop the darkness from leaking from my room the sun disappeared your white carpets turned grey and somber your joy tainted.

* * *

But the lover of knowledge who is obtrusive with his eyes – how could he see more of all things than their foregrounds? But you, O Zarathustra, wanted to see the ground and background of all things; hence you must climb over yourself – upward, up until even your stars are under you!

I return to you ashamed I have not conquered my disease I am weak I have failed. This time papa silent looks at me resentment in his eyes maman takes charge finding strength in my vulnerability. You are not made for this world papa says we will fight this maman says here is what you should not eat.

I am climbing I will reach the stars I will uncover the pain I will heal myself. My resolve strong I face the world tie rockets to my fingers learn to climb mountains I stand at the peak and peer into the abyss.

I see you. You are the abyss. You tell me not to look down you say the ground is far away keep your head up work hard forget. I do not tell you I am a master of forgetting I do not tell you I have shares in the warehouse of forgetting it comes in dyes I put it in my bath bathe in it let it change me let it wrap itself around me. I do not tell you it is lethal contaminated worn out. I do not tell you it is killing me to forget.

I try not to cry in front of you I try not to include you in my pain I try to be invisible around you I want you to forgive me my pain I want your love. You cannot love me you have brought me into this world I am a reminder of yourself you cannot bear my pain you despise me. I crawl into my bed muffle my sobs with my pillow I cry myself to sleep. My tears enrage you you scream go somewhere else I cannot help you. I have not asked for your help I want your love you have no love for me I am a wanderer I leave once more.

That night I run my body covered lightly with my faded nightshirt the world grey with the fallen sun. My feet against the cement I run and run I am running away from you you will not find me I will not burden you with my pain.

You are my pain.

* * *

Every day I wander in and out of your room. Every day we invent a language we build a chest that will contain my wanderings. Every day I wander with you.

Analysis ends today I have opened my book to you have showed you the images in my mind. Today we pile my wanderings neatly into the left-hand corner of the pack I carry on my back trying to hold the words that will compose me. I leave I wander through the streets your words still moist in my mouth the order in the pack dispersed with every movement.

When I read to you I feel you swallow my words I feel you feeling the scar under my breast I feel you feeling me. When I read to you I feel you piling the words into the pack that is our creation. You ask me silently how many we will keep how many we will throw violently out of the window into the void that is the universe. Into the universe we disperse words of victimization boring meaningless words I have been fed words that do not belong to me. You know when you listen to me which words are my own.

Three o'clock says my watch the afternoon is falling in around me. Analysis is over and I am alone again sitting still in the middle of my narcissism. Three o'clock and time is ticking by the seconds of my life multiplying I am getting older soon I will be old. Three o'clock and I look forward to the wrinkles around my eyes the wrinkles that will show life as it has passed by leaving its mark on my body. Three o'clock and I have lived.

The hour passes like the mistral it blows on us as we search through my pack together it disrobes us messes our hair cools us off. Bits of wind get caught in our shoes in our zippers in the space between our fingers bits that will disperse as we move through the day. Today I write the wind into my book as I wander through the words. Today I write my wandering.

* * *

Nightmares

Last night I dream of you my lover. I dream a nightmare. We are in a car you with another one you make love with me tell me you love me you stay with her. I ask you to come to me to talk with me you say we have nothing to talk about. You said you loved me I say it is your imagination you say. I look at you my eyes well up with tears I am sure it happened I am sure it is real. You say it is not real. Your word is stronger than mine you have the voice I fall silent I am drowning in my sleep. Perhaps this is a nightmare I think. In my sleep I turn to you my eyes still closed I say hold me. You wake at once your strong arms wrapped around me we sing superhero songs imagine balloons lifting us high into the sky. It is a nightmare you say it is not real.

I lie awake afraid to close my eyes I think of the lives lived in my dreams my fears so real. I remember my dreams they populate my days every memory of you a nightmare.

Morning rises you open your eyes it was a dream you say. You are my lover not the one of my nightmares your body takes on the form of my fears. Our bodies linked we lie entwined holding our breath we do not see the minutes walking by.

You are my lover I have known you all my life I have known you since last night when you pulled me out of the grip of monsters. You have not left me like you warned.

Every day we have come closer our love stronger. Sometimes I know you. Sometimes I dream of you.

This is a love story, a story about love. You are my story.

* * *

Christmas comes and leaves we do not spend much time together we stay apart I am afraid. The thread that holds us together is at its limit thin and worn the connections full of static. Our love is strong my fear is stronger will you hurt me leave me when I am not looking? Every morning I get up early build my armor soon I will be impenetrable. You watch me build you bring me stones and ice and iron you watch me as I set the time for my departure. Christmas season almost over we sleep together I dream of discarding my walls I dream of you. You talk to me sometimes in my sleep you come to me in my dreams. I want to know will we stay together I want to know will I ever want to leave I want to know will I suffer I want to know. You are my lover you have no answers you wrap yourself around me stay close you say.

* * *

Today I write on the bus my writing bumpy my thoughts vivid with nightmares and madness. I am seventeen and the food left in my stomach after throwing up feeds my nightmares makes them grow one into another. When I don't throw up I sit in a chair by the window and I look at the blank images forming in my head that will be my nightmares when I lay my body next to yours. You do not understand my world my nightmares scare you they wake you in the night you want to hold me close my skin burns at your touch. When we are close the monsters grow you will not let me go will not let me escape you are afraid. For thirteen days I sit in the chair by the window I wait for you to bring me roses an apology for gripping the life out of me when I dreamt of you last night. You come too late my food already flushed down the toilet we do not speak I have no words until my nightmares speak again.

I ask you to leave. Your presence gone the nightmares fade the days fade into night I don't turn on the light I burn candles by my bed. You have been gone three days three months three years your body still sown into mine I spend my days cutting the cloth that formed us. I cannot walk you took my legs when you left. In your suitcase you packed my nightmares my right breast ten toes you wanted to remember me. I did not stop you. I lie in bed I cannot walk cannot feed myself you have taken my life.

Last night I had a nightmare. In my nightmare you left.

* * *

Christmas once again my body thin I will not eat my starvation entices you keeps you away. You still walk on my body try to hand me pieces of myself try to come back. You push yourself into my nightmares. I run from you I starve myself I am making myself invisible soon you will not see me. It is Christmas and I am alone.

I meet her through a friend she invites me for New Year's dinner a feast of sauces meats and vegetables there are many of us at the table. I come to you dressed in my favourite clothes a dark green silk velvet vest with gold buttons I feel your eyes rest on my body. Quietly I eat my food I listen to strangers talk I watch you with my hand as I lick the sauce from my fingers I feel you next to me as I pass the vegetables I touch you with my desire. I feel the blood in my legs I feel my right breast I feel alive I watch you smell you feel you with my body.

The New Year here you speak to me ask about my passion I take your head in my hands press it against the creases the crevices the gaps the porous holes that form my body the contours that invent my paintings that write my stories I look into your bright blue eyes sparkling with my gaze I know you understand. Your fingers caress the empty space within the gaps I exist through your touch you will be my next painting my new story I feel the writing on my body you leave your mark. I don't ask you who you are I long to touch your thick black hair the bump on your stomach the child growing inside. Come back you say. Yes I say.

Every week I go to you we cook together our concoctions how we grow our connection. I can almost keep them down. We are building a creature through which we will communicate a creature that will be our own. Soon I know I will have to leave to allow your baby to emerge in solitude far from my nightmares. But today the time has not yet come. I lie next to you under the soft blanket you caress my face touch my pain put clean sheets on the bed I sleep next to you my dreams calm.

Three months pass it is time to leave I hold you close we say goodbye. You do not understand. In the plane I am alone I see no one they do not see my pain they do not see my heart as it shrivels inside my chest. I will see you again I tell myself this is a love story I tell myself surely it will have a happy ending.

* * *

I write to you my writing fragmented bumpy this is my nightmare the fingerprints on my body as I allow my mind to drift into sleep. I have travelled far have arrived in a new city have found a new place from which to murder my nightmare to keep it from invading me when I am awake.

Last night my nightmare devastating it was too close to my life my fears revealed stark in my sleep I dreamt of you. Your face next to mine it broke my heart to feel a hole where your desire might have been. When I woke you encased me within your body I climbed still further inside you I curled into a gap hoping to find a clue to your desire. You give me no clues desire has no answers love exists only as we create it. You cannot comfort me in my sorrow. You hold me close. These are your fears you say.

Days tangled with misunderstandings I introduce myself to you a new introduction each day. You are my lover yours is the body I wake next to from my troubled sleep yours is the body I long for the body I fear. You leave me in the mornings travel to a world separate from my own return different in the evenings. Sun sinking behind the tall buildings I see you walk toward my door as I capture you from my balcony. On the stairs I hear your step. Sometimes you fly into my arms. I prepare for you each night I wait for you my body tense with your arrival I anticipate you.

You are not my nightmare you listen when I speak you see my body as it lies under yours as I lie beside you as I tie you to the bed my lover the prize of my desire. You are not my nightmare you do not hit me do not ignore me do not blame me. And yet our space is the well from which monsters emerge. Your body strong and lithe you are the guard who stands by the well who waits for monsters prepared to choke them with your silent rage. But they see you and stay away. You turn your head your thoughts wander you caress my hand softly and they emerge a battlefield I see them they creep toward me already consuming me you cannot see them. You see the tension on my face the breaking of the skin around my eyes fear erupting from within me they have fooled you again. I cry out my anguish distressing to your ears my body writhing you are my monster I cannot see you your body distorted by my fear. Your touch contains me you build a garden for my fear sing to me kiss my forehead already glistening with sweat. I am here with you you say hold on tight we will terrify them together and we scream my agony AAAAHHHH!

We are two we are one our difference creates us we grow together we are lovers.

Today I fight the monsters alone. I keep watch I do not see them the sun is high. They usually emerge from the forbidding purple that lines the darkness but sometimes they are in the afternoon shadows. I must keep watch. The clothes I wear today will surprise them. I am wearing holes against my skin black lace cut into flowers my body showing through. I do not see them yet.

* * *

I leave you. I leave your sparkling eyes blue jewels on your face curly black hair I leave you behind I miss you as the days draw longer shadows on my skin. My plane flies high into the sky you are shrinking underneath me disappearing. On the ground at your feet I can see a crystal forming the colours of my body I have left behind for you. Bright orange holds your joy close to your heart you must not cry your baby is too young for the taste of salt tears. Bright orange your spirit is clothed your child kicking happily under your heart your blue eyes bright.

I leave you don't want to contaminate you with my nightmares don't want to scare your baby still unformed. He will grow up he will learn to fight monsters he will grow strong and I will visit you again.

* * *

I sit next to people I have not met they do not look at me they do not know they are protecting me from my nightmares. They look away. I have travelled to a big city a place where everyone walks alone furtive looks escaping from beneath their sunglasses. Will you stay long the woman in charge asks. As long as it takes I say quietly. She does not hear me there are no ears left in this city of a thousand walls.

* * *

I leave you to return to the nightmare of my childhood the one about the man with the red hair the one who chases me. I will meet this man I will kill him with my bare hands and then I will return to you we will be a family you and me and the little one not yet born.

I have found my revenge I plan it every day practice it every night before I go to sleep. I will be you I tell him I will overcome you I will become you. I fall asleep I look for you but you do not come. Every night I wait for you my legs strong from training I wait for you I will run you down I will terrorize you I will make you wake every night your body drenched with sweat.

You have not returned new nightmares have emerged I fight each one with vigour every new one recreating an old one my body tense with fear. You will not enter me I tell the monsters before I go to sleep. I clutch your hand I will know that I am dreaming I will wake I will not dream. Some nights my body wakes terror filling my bones consuming me some nights I sleep a gentle sleep.

I have not yet returned to you your baby big already. I am still waiting.

* * *

Walls

There are four walls I can feel them pressing in on my body I am trapped. You lie on the ground close to me you sleep I am alone in my silence you are my captor. Rain falls thick on the roof encasing me I want to run there is nowhere to go.

I am twenty-five and a thousand I do not want to return to that time when I must wait for you to come to me where you hold the reigns on my freedom. I don't want to be two again. When you sleep I am the only one alive the world dead around me I choke in my solitude.

You do not suspect me do not know that your sleep is tying me to you as maman's sleep arrested me made me long for her to wake. You woke up but it was too late I was already old grown up I no longer needed you to be awake. The afternoons interminable the house quiet please don't fall asleep.

You shut your eyes and drift into a sleep I cannot penetrate I live with you eat with you sleep with you I cannot see within your dreams I cannot take the potion that helps you sink into your world of dreams I cannot sleep my nightmares keep me awake I lie still. Your breath regular I know you have left me your body next to mine so far away I am alone I cannot sleep.

Time passes my body accustomed to insomnia I no longer fight to find that state you so eagerly fall into. The hours of the night are my private hours my time to dream to lie awake. The sun rises I hear the world awakening my eyes get heavy you rise I fall into a slumber from which only night can wake me I am seventeen.

* * *

My life is full of walls to encage walls to protect. In the evening before supper I build my walls one stone at a time. I am building my cage. Soon your sleep will no longer penetrate my walls I will be my own company in my solitude you will no longer exist. I do not show you my efforts you are afraid of walls you pretend to stay awake you are afraid to lose me you have already lost me your world so far away from mine. I am angry with you for your sleep I envy you I long to lay my head down on the pillow next to yours to share your happy dreams. Behind my eyes I see nightmares. In front of the nightmares I build walls.

I leave you no longer live with you eat with you sleep with you I have my own bed I sleep alone. The curtains drawn I do not know day or night sometimes I sleep sometimes I lie awake and watch the colours of my curtain dim with the setting sun. I am seventeen I am eighteen I am nineteen I have lost my sleep I gave it to the raboo who broke through the shutters of my childhood. Beside my bed I have a candle I read Anaïs Nin my world an exhausted sleepless fantasy. She lives inside my head I speak to no one they all sleep when I am awake my body tired and restless.

Today I borrow the words from my body to tell you my story while you sleep. Today I long to sleep your sleep.

* * *

I wake your body rubbing against mine my mind numbed under your weight I say nothing. Your hands exploring my body I remember the marks left by the last explorer. I am twenty-five I am two and a thousand I have no words to stop you I say nothing. My body limp my mind drifts I imagine my lover I imagine a place that is my own I imagine my escape I say nothing.

You moan your pleasure you speak of love and desire the scars on my body wet with pain I do not let you in you do not see me I am invisible small beneath your weight. I am two I am three I am eleven I am thirteen I am twenty-five and a thousand.

I murmur something the words screaming in my head. The last brick! I forgot a brick! I let you in you saw that brick the one I didn't fasten the one I set on top waiting for a rainy day waiting for a sad time to pin it down on top of all of the other bricks the one that would have safe-guarded me. My wall was not yet finished. And you saw.

Your hands reach for the last brick the one that covers my heart and you pull. Your arms weakened by desire you cannot detach the pain that holds the brick tightly along the scar under my breast. You pretend not to notice that I am not there that you are sleeping with my pain. I hold my breath you fall asleep exhausted by the effort. I will not sleep again.

* * *

Today time crawls through me. I am far away from you the bearer of my pain. She says you have assaulted me. I have no words for your performance. I have no words. My body cries in pain. Awake in the night I remember you as time reveals itself to me. I taste your breath against my lips I dream of you my eyes wide open afraid of sleep.

Today time crawls through me. I try to make excuses for you and you and you the ones who have owned my body the ones who have broken through my flesh. I speak for you discount your actions reveal your secrets to no one. I am your captor faithful to your actions I do not speak.

Today time crawls through me. I lie my back curled up against you my lover. You see the silent screams written on my skin you weep for me your hands gently massaging away your touch. Your voice coarse with anger you speak of rape you speak the violence of the words unspoken on my body you speak my voice. My words slow and unsure I try to protect you I can feel my breath caught in my throat death is sitting in my soul I lack the words for your protection. For four years I have stopped rehearsing them. For four years no one has touched my body. For four years I have remembered. For four years I have protected you. For four years I have not spoken my body starved and waiting to die.

I cannot eat you feed me quietly first with love then with pineapple to sweeten the terror then with anger. The anger is too big to swallow I feel it as it submerges me I gasp I cannot breathe you hold me tight swallow you say you will breathe again swallow you will live swallow! I cannot swallow all of it spit some out you pushe it back into my mouth one piece at a time. This is the beginning you say there will be more this anger will flush through you quickly offset by the softness of my caress and the sweetness of my love.

At night I dream another nightmare. I am in a Nazi camp they have captured us I am guilty. The man in charge will give my lover his life in exchange for my body. I refuse. In terror I wake turn to you the tears stopping my words I tell you I have sentenced you to die. You refused to give your body you say you have chosen life this is the beginning. On the night table you reach for the silver spoon and feed me a few bites of anger. I go back to sleep.

Today I build a boundary so high you will not see over the top even from the moon you will not find me. One by one I undo the bricks of the incomplete wall that stole my voice and let you in. Today I build a boundary to keep you out. Today I build a world for myself. Today I write my book.

* * *

Darkness

Night has come; now all fountains speak more loudly. And my soul too is a fountain. Night has come; only now all the songs of lovers awaken. And my soul too is the song of a lover. Something unstilled, unstillable is within me; it wants to be voiced. A craving for love is within me; it speaks the language of love.

Night falls and I come to you. We are lovers the night short we do not sleep my fingers discovering you beneath my touch. In silence we meet the night together we sew the words into one-another the words that will rise with the morning sun. I feel the quiver of your skin taut under my silence. You are my lover. We are the night.

* * *

Today I wake from a long night I feel the sun shine softly on my body I wake to its glow I am alive. Today I am twenty-five and a thousand I have woken many times have felt the sun have lifted my heavy body from the sheets have walked the day beside me I have lived. Today I live again my face tense with the life that was yesterday tense with the expectation of tomorrow as time passes through me.

In my heart I am alone. The night too long I wake early the dawn still dull the grass wet with dew against my bare body the blades of grass each a word as they caress the soles of my feet. I gather my words and begin to speak. After the night there is much to say.

Today I am no longer seventeen no longer fifteen no longer three. I am moving from the darkness of my life soon I will reach the depth of the abyss soon I will begin to climb my head peering over the edge soon my life will begin. Already I have lived many lives many more than twenty-five and perhaps less than a thousand and soon I will live again. The night will fall and I will wake listening for my lover's words whispered in my ear listening to his body as it approaches mine listening to the night as it turns into day.

The darkest hour comes more than once. I am tortured by the night that lives within me the night that will not turn into day. I am seventeen I am eighteen I am nineteen I am two I live the night my mask already worn and tattered by my excursions into the light that exposes me into the darkness that conceals me. Desperately I cling to life I travel the darkness sleep through the rising sun wake to sleep again. Every day I purge the sunlight that won't sink through the scars left on my skin. You have blocked the sun. I am drowning I am succumbing to the darkness.

I dream of sleep my eyes half open the calm refuses to descend I am slipping off the edge soon I will fall deep into the abyss. I peer into the depths my voice still there is no language in the bottom of the pit no language in the womb of death. I long to impose silence on my tortured body. I scream silent screams. I dream of night engulfing me I long for colour the colour of my blood I long for death I long for silence. I have no words no body no desire I want to plunge into the slippery crimson of my death I am standing at the edge of the precipice reaching down I am falling.

The fall long and slow I feel my body fly I am light as I peel the words from my skin the warm red liquid encasing me. I am sitting at the bottom the pool of blood surrounding me I watch for no one I see nothing I do not speak I cannot hear. Today I will sleep without a kiss from you I will not sing myself to sleep I will fall slowly into bliss I am falling.

* * *

I wake to you peering down into my eyes I curse my failure the words stuck in my throat my body bandaged. The bandage conceals my scars no one can see them they are hidden in my misery. I have failed my wakefulness a symbol of the pain I will never be able to hide. You look reproachfully into my eyes your gaze fixed on my bandages we have no words I have bled my voice. I want to ask did you save my blood did you find the words that peeled off my body forming the pool of cherries in which I lay have you come to me with my soul will you replace the words I can no longer speak have you brought my mask? You say nothing you cannot hear my words I have left my voice behind.

Time no longer passes through me my body gone I lie on a white bed watch the ceiling as the hours stand still I wait for no one. They don't turn off the light they think they have destroyed the night that lurks inside my scars I lie awake the spotlight glaring against my face that never moves I am dead. I have no nightmares I am dead like the night that never falls they have stolen the blood have stopped the flow have taken the silence along with the words.

They feed me I do not throw up they follow me to the bathroom watch me at night tie me to my bed she is dangerous they say dangerous to herself I am not dangerous I have fallen into the abyss where there is no life please let go of me. They do not let go it is their job to sustain life I am captive in the maze of their undertaking. They do not notice that time stands still that I am disappearing today I am missing the nails on my fingers tomorrow perhaps I will lose my toes and then my legs. I lie in bed I cannot walk the weight too much for my body weak with silence they scold me for my laziness they bandage my scars they pull me out of bed they pretend that I am not invisible they pretend that I am alive.

* * *

This is a love story, a story about love. I sit next to you my lover sick with the memory of how the scars heal and the pain hides underneath. This is a love story, a story about love. I sit next to you my lover and we share my pain your face distorted with the memory we cannot share.

* * *

The scar is healing blood no longer dripping from my wrist I have not succeeded now I wear sunglasses against the sun. I live in darkness. My body heavy with scar tissue I starve myself soon there will be nothing but scars nothing to remind me of the softness that surrounds the broken skin nothing to remind me of my body before it was ravaged by you. Soon I will be nothing but the pain you have caused me soon my body will disappear. Soon we will be one.

The scar is healing I remove the bandage I pretend I never longed for liquid crimson I pretend you have not killed me I pretend I am alive. I travel far and wide find a new mask no one will recognize fit it tightly against my face not even you will know me now I do not know myself. I am a slave to you I will fight to the death for your recognition I will make myself more and more foreign this will be our duel come and find me if you can. Every day my body thinner I stand shivering limp with exhaustion you do not see me I am disappearing.

I rape my body starve it abuse it hate it more each day I eat your flesh the memory of you my sustenance as we fight to the death. Desire is the desire for the other there is no other only the other within myself my body split I am the victim of my body scratched by your claws.

I walk my head high no one dares to look at me they are afraid of the terrible starvation they witness. My starvation is my salvation. I am not starving I tell myself I am free from you I have won I am dead. At night I go to bed my body tired bones weary of life my hands do not reach for the softness concealed in the folds of my body. I have killed my desire.

* * *

This is a love story, a story about love. My body marked and scarred and ravaged by violence is also my body awake and hungry for love. You are with me my lover I tell you my story you watch my body bleed. The words coagulate the flow slows down you wipe away the redness that stains your life. I leave traces of my pain behind I see it in your face when I speak to you you see it in my body as I lean toward you we talk little of our pain we invent a new language we invent our joy. We do not erase the pain we write it slowly softly on each other's body we moan with pleasure as the writing reveals us in our ecstasy we lick the streams of tears left behind in our pleasure so close to sadness so close to joy we love each other.

Today I tell you a story you listen to my eyes as they cloud over you talk to my heart as it constricts you touch my stomach where it hurts you listen. I tell you about the scar I tell you about my shame I tell you about the crimson pool I sometimes yearn for I tell you about the slave I conquered as I starved myself to death. I have grown enormous no longer starved my body repels me often hungry with desire. Your hand on the soft curve of my stomach you whisper through my skin you touch me with your desire. I look for a happy ending. This is a love story, a story about love.

Night has fallen. In my heart I feel the darkness. To-night I hold the darkness in my hands. Tonight as I fall asleep my hand reaches for the softness hidden among the scars. Tonight as darkness descends I feel pleasure.

The scar is healed there is no longer sign of blood. Every day I am stronger every day I write more words every day I write my story. The fiction of my words release me my voice clearer my lungs deeper soon I will speak my name. The time is not yet come for me to reveal myself. The time is not yet come for me to name you.

One day I will purge you you will ooze out of my pores your name will ring so loud you will hear nothing but yourself my anger deafening I will condemn you you will suffer my shame you will swallow my body you will choke on my scars. One day I will scream my pain and you will hear me.

The wind blows it caresses the redness of my hair the curls growing slowly it reminds me of the softness I used to crave of the dreams left balancing in the air of the words I could not speak. I cut my curls I wanted you to see my face I wanted you to feel the hardness you have created I wanted you to see the beauty you ignored I wanted you to see the life you tried to take. Every day the wind blows more hair as my hair grows and the curls try to return. Every day I come closer to the end. Every day I wonder if there will be a happy ending. Every day I write my body.

* * *

The Fracture

You bring me into the world. You look at me carefully. Two legs two arms a nose a mouth two ears. I am acceptable to you. I am not a mutant.

You bring me into the world. You look at me carefully. You check between my legs under my belly button on the curve of my breast. You are looking for a fracture. You see nothing.

Look more carefully and you will see that your creation is full of fractures. The nose small and straight conceals smells you have not dreamed of. The mouth closed and soft holds secrets you cannot know. The breast smooth and round hides a scar as wide as your life. I am fractured and you cannot see me. You have not created me.

* * *

I am preparing to break open. I am ready for the eruption. Every day I think about you every day I create you once more every day I invent myself every day I write my body.

I search back into time I place myself deep within my mother's womb I listen to the words spoken I listen to the music of your body I am your body. You drop me into the world I cry and scream my awakening violent and terrifying I begin to live. You must let go of me I am no longer your body I see my toes my fingers I feel the air cool the sun warm the days corroding my skin I am my body. You look at me sometimes you see me we share a broken heart we each carry a portion of the other in our breast.

Today I take back my heart. I place it under my breast I hold it gently between trembling hands. It bleeds where it has been broken. It bleeds where it has felt pain. It bleeds where it has felt joy. My heart bleeds as I insert it already fractured into my chest.

Today I am twenty-five and a thousand and I have my own heart. I pretend the blue stains on my body are veins I pretend the blood that erupts from within me each month is not the blood of my conception I pretend I stand strong and confident in the world with my own heart.

In time I see that I am not linear. I have been old and young sometimes both in a day I have needed you I have run from you I have been you you have been me. Today I write the story of time as it passes through me. Today I place my body in your hands. Today I write my book.

I am two years old and we are flying away together to another place where we will find happiness. I am two years old and I know we will not find ourselves in that other place I am two years old and a thousand I am fifteen and two seventeen and two twenty-two and two twenty-five and a thousand I still have not found what I am looking for. I am twenty-five and a thousand and I am no longer searching.

I want to tell you a story. I have promised you a love story, a story about love. Today I will keep my promise.

* * *

I am old now the scars on my body thick with time I am looking for life. Time is heavy it holds me sometimes I writhe with time sometimes it sets me free sometimes I fly. I am twenty now twenty-one twenty-two twenty-three and I watch the world as it marches by me I feel the world as I carry it in my arms as I glide on its surface.

Thousands of seconds have left tiny riffs on my skin I am wrinkled by time I have seen walls in many rooms I have watched the world from the inside. I am a spectator of the world I watch myself from the room I have created. From this one purple and dark green I keep an eye on you I look at your face I see you twitch as I threaten to speak your name. From this room I conceal my identity. My body covered by the colours I have chosen I wait for you I am the victor here do you dare enter? Come and I will tell you a story. Once I have told you the story we will look for the scissors I keep in the drawer of the hard wood desk and we will sever the ties that hold the story in place we will fracture it and together we will look to see what grows from within the fissures we have created together. Together we will write a love story. And then I will take the scissors and with one sharp blow to your heart I will enter you. The blood from your fractured heart will not flow it will not pour. Your heart is dry already severed by my story you have died your fingers still holding the pages of my book your palms burned where you tried to touch my body.

Slowly I will tear the corners of the pages I will hold them to my heart for they are mine. My words no longer in your hands you will fade your fingers detached from your body you will fall apart fractured beyond repair I will have killed you. And with the remains of your fractured body I will paint you blood red and black onto my wall. My silence will be broken.

* * *

Today I am twenty and I watch the world from the separate place I have chosen for my healing. I do not yet know that to heal myself I will have to walk into the world to inhabit it to feel it with my body to cover myself with its blood. Today I am safe where there are many walls to keep me from the world that tears at my soul.

For three weeks I have not thrown up the bandages on my body now removed I am listening to the wisdom shared with me from within these walls. You structure my life here I know when to rise when to eat when to listen when to speak when to sleep. Here I am safe.

For three weeks the world leaves no marks on my body. For three weeks I sleep without nightmares. For three weeks I do not dream. I am quiet in my soul my body at rest I am healing myself seduced my the silence that reigns distanced from the pain. You speak to me your voice soft you ask me to talk you say words will help to heal the festering sores beneath my skin. Every day I feel speech closer to my throat soon I will speak out soon I will rupture the silence.

Four weeks now and I speak my first word. We are sitting in a circle and a woman cries out demons swimming in her body I watch her squeal with pain as the beast draws blood rips out her heart it falls to the ground at my feet I scream in terror I have spoken. I run to the corner I become an animal my yelps deafening to human ears my pain inhuman I cry my rage. You approach me the one I trust take me into your arms I hear your music in my ears you soothe me cry you say you have spoken your pain you are alive you have survived it once the memory will not kill you you will live. I do not hear your words I hear your closeness I feel the softness of your flesh her arms wrapped around my head I feel your body against mine. I scream my voice harsh I stop a second the room is silent I hear myself for the first time in weeks. My eyes now wide open I watch the faces watching me they are not looking at me they are looking at their own pain they do not mock me they feel the world tearing at their skin they feel their bodies loud with the noise of terror they are alive with my screams they thank me with their eyes. Today I have been here four weeks. Within these walls white rooms uncontaminated air I will find life and then they will throw me back into the world where my screams will not be heard where the silence will not hold the notes of my pain stiff in the air where no one will listen. Today I have been here four weeks. I am afraid they will soon send me back.

The days are shorter now time fractured by my words I speak in tongues waterfalls canyons emerging from my pain. Morning until night they include me in their circles they give me canvasses to paint they introduce me to myself they listen to the volcanoes erupting from my silence they wipe the puss as it leaks from my sores. I am getting stronger I can walk on my legs still weak sometimes I leave my room to watch the others swim in the pool I play jacks with the one who is my sister I steal a pear and exchange it for a glass of milk and then I laugh. My laugh startles me I am afraid they will have heard I am afraid they will send me back I am scared.

You invite me into your office a time unscheduled the others together in the common room you say you want to speak to me. Soon it will be time to leave you say you are much stronger already. I look around your office see the painting on the wall signed by my name I cry tears streaming down my face. One by one you watch the tears as they swim into the folds of my body as they heal the rage I have been learning to speak you will know when it's time you say you will tell me when you are ready to leave.

In the common room the others look at me they see the canyons in my skin dug by the tears they do not ask. We sit together a room full of silence. I am the youngest here my body not yet sagging with my pain others will leave as well some have gone already soon it will be my turn.

I join their circle a few more times my nights alive with dreams I feel the world as it enters my body I know that soon I will return. Under my bed I hide my suitcase packed now since Monday it is Friday today I will tell them. Quietly I leave the room that has been my haven for many days I walk down the hall where she is playing cards where she is reading where her eyes are shut tightly with memories. I watch them they do not see me I have changed my body already far from theirs I walk to her office and knock on the door. You welcome me. This time your eyes are wet as you accept my last painting. You walk me to the door. Today my life begins.

* * *

The Journey

You trace the outline of my face with your index finger. The red of my hair leaves a slight tint of colour on the tip of your finger. You use the colour to draw my eyes. You paint them wide open. You find it difficult to draw my nose, first you make it broad, then pointed, then a mixture of the two. My mouth emerges on its own already bursting with words.

You place the first wrinkle of our journey between the palms of your hands. You hold it tightly making sure not to apply too much pressure making sure not to iron it out. You place the wrinkle where you think my body should be. You watch as the wrinkle grows. You watch as my body takes form.

You take my body into your arms. You caress the skin already wrinkled with time. We begin our journey.

* * *

As I walk away I leave a trail of small white pills a trail of nurses of unfinished paintings a trail of care and love my trail longer and longer as the distance thickens between my body and the palm trees that surround the building with the white walls and the programmed days. Outside in the bright glare of the sun the world watches me as I reenter it the ground sagging beneath my feet.

The days pass the world grows every day the battles more eloquent the joys more intense the violence more brutal. Today a thousand years have passed since that day when the ground seemed new to the tread of my shoes. Today my shoes are worn down. Today the smells of life are mingled smells of fresh bread smells of late night conversations smells of vomit smells of triumph. The day I left the hospital it was the smell of the world I noticed. I was accosted by the smell of complications by the smell of uncertainty. As I walked through streets in my new shoes I gathered in my small bag all of the smells I had grown accustomed to ignoring all of the smells that distinguished the world from the safe place of my confinement. And I learned to breathe.

Today my apartment is dark with the smell of vomit. Today my life is dark with the smell of memory. Today the world is dark with the smell of confusion. On my body I see the mark of last night's dream in which I was the tyrant in which my lover was the abuser in which I raped myself in which my lover raped me. From my dream I woke with the dingy smell of misery I woke with the knowledge that I make the choice to live I woke with the terror of possibility and I could not go back to sleep.

My fingers are slow on the keys my mind dimmer than the screen. The words I pluck from my skin are not the words I want to write not the sentences I thought I would compose. I am appalled by my choices I want to change my words I want to reach to the thesaurus and couch the intensity of my self-destruction I want to stop writing my body I want to walk off the path I have chosen I want a ticket to leave my journey behind.

Please sir I say to the train conductor if I could only leave the train of thought for a few days I would surely long to return. He looks at my ticket pulls out his magnifying glass and solemnly shakes his head. I'm afraid you have a one-way ticket ma'am he says and I want to destroy him to erase him from my vocabulary. Smell my hands I scream can't you smell the rancid vomit still clinging to the fingers with which I type my manuscript? Can't you smell the rotting flesh of my body? But he is already busy with another customer a woman crying holding a child in her arms a woman holding her own body small and vulnerable between trembling hands pleading with the conductor to hold the child for just a moment. I watch as he refuses his face made of stone.

My bathroom is daunting the smell of vomit hanging in the air the smell of past experience the smell of your hands on my body the smell of your laughter the smell of your sarcasm the smell of your destruction the smell of life undigested. I know I must clean it up I know I can't let you see the state of my insides spread on the toilet on the floor I know I must retain the illusion that I am empty. My emptiness preserves your life allows you to continue to live in your fantasy the illusion of calm and comfort and fullness. Teeth marks on my hand the taste of blood lingering in my mouth you do not know that I have revealed myself disgusting to you that I am the monster you hide inside your body that I am the breath you breathe that I am choking in my vomit.

This is my journey. These are the contours of life on my body the redness that interrupts our communication the pointed spears of my soul you never lean against the quills that would puncture you if you had the courage to approach me. My body still sore from throwing up I wait for you to contact me I wait for you to tell me my next move. I remove the receiver from its cradle. This journey has already lasted too long. Today I will not hear your voice.

* * *

This a love story, a story about a love. How can I write a love story when all I feel is the pain in my stomach? How can I tell you about love when I long to find a love that doesn't make my heart quiver? How can I admit to loving when my body is frozen in a state of self-destruction? How can I speak of a journey of the body when there is an eternal return of the same terror of the same death a nihilistic eternal return of the same?

Hanging on my window I see the watch my talisman it reads two-thirty the same time it stopped at yesterday. Hanging in my closet I see the twenty-shirts waiting for you unsullied by life. Written on my heart broken and bleeding I hear your name I listen to the memory of you I smell you the smell of vomit still hanging on my skin.

I want to tell you a love story but every word I write today leaves a burning sensation in my body. I feel the churning of my ulcer I feel sleep descending into my eyes denying your presence I hear my ears listening for your step I feel your body assaulting mine.

In the intersection of moment and place I search for a door. I want to open it and find myself. When I find myself I will pull from the inside to find the words to speak. In the intersection of moment and place I will find my voice and with my voice I will speak of my journey.

My journey began seventeen chapters ago seventeen days ago seventeen years ago seventeen centuries ago. My journey began the first time I reached for the handle on the door that opened to a question mark. My journey began with the first question that stopped frozen in my throat. My journey began with the first word I was unable to speak.

As my feet hit the pavement after the soft carpets of the hospital ward I begin the journey I have already begun. With every new step I hear another word. In the pad I keep in my front pocket I record the words I find. In the pack I wear on my back I try to keep them in order. One by one I add them to my story. Beside the words I keep the punctuation. I want to use these newfound words I want to ask you why I want to say why weren't you there I want to say why didn't you tell me I could say no? Madly I scratch away words you taught me words that mean nothing words that say give me what you think I deserve words that say I am not worth anything words that say nothing. On top of my old words I scribble new words that gather as medleys of the smells and tastes of the world around me. For the first time in weeks I am out-side. For the first time in weeks noise surrounds me that is more than the screams inside my head.

I am lost in the maze of the world. I have nowhere to turn the streets all look the same every question mark still unanswered every exclamation lacks a voice. I walk until my feet are too tired to carry me. I long to be carried I long to find a soft space where I will be safe. I miss the walls of my confinement.

* * *

In the middle of the labyrinth I gasp for air and find you. You are my lover. With you I retrace my steps. Together we look for the door that will open to the next maze from which we will escape again. Our journey is incomplete. Together we trace and retrace one-another. To you I tell my story. Side by side we walk creating many sets of foot-prints. Sometimes we lie together and hold the world at bay sometimes I tell you secrets that cause avalanches. It is you I find today in the middle of the labyrinth.

From my front pocket from the pack on my back from behind my knee I pull out the words I have captured. In order to read them you close your eyes and extend your hand. I feel you as your skin touches mine. I feel your body warm against the thickness of place and moment as they meet.

You come to me today as you have many times before. You come to me in the middle of a memory. You lend me your feet and together we scrape across the pavement on the first day of my freedom. Together we smell the fresh bread. Together we clean up the vomit I don't want you to see. Your tongue reaches out to catch my uneven sobs and you listen to my despair. You listen to the words I have learned today you listen to failure. You have not failed you say look at the word the one in red the first one on your list the one you learned somewhere in that other memory. Rape. I see the red I cannot see the word I am afraid to look. I am tired it is easier to carry the pain in my body easier than to extend it to you the one for whom I have had to learn this word. In bold letters you retrace the word onto my body. Again and again I feel the stark letters against my skin my body echoing its pain as it re-members. You hold me your arms tight around me you tell me that I have not failed you say that failure is one word we will not write down you are angry at the world I can hear the anger in the hardness of the silence that surrounds us.

We lie together on my bed our bodies entwined you trace a box on my left breast and name it anger. One by one you brush away the sobs already hardened on my body your fingers lightly stroking my skin as you soften the tears in order to place them in the box you have just created. The tears are flowing I can feel the wetness of my body as I approach you. My lips press against yours you close the box hold the anger you say and direct it out-ward. I feel your hands your grip hardening our bodies quickening with desire.

My body tender my stomach sore my throat aching with self-destruction I long for you. You are my lover we make love careful not to seal the box you traced on my left breast careful not to erase the anger I am learning to speak. I am confused by my desire for you confused by my nipples erect by the urgency I feel I am confused by the door we have opened together in the intersection of place and moment I am confused by the diversity of emotions love creates I am confused by love.

The hospital rooms white and square did not prepare me for a journey in which you would inspire desire beside tears closeness beside anger vulnerability beside terror.

They did not warn me that with you I would create a language in which I would include the words of our creation as well as the words of our destruction. Together we write rape into my life in bright red letters together we travel the anger I am discovering together we experience the tender moments of love.

I make love to you my lover and I know I am sharing with you the darkest secret of my soul. With you I am sharing my desire unleashed and vulnerable. You do not ask me to be close to you you do not tell me who I am you do not tell me how to feel you listen when I speak you listen to the music of my words you listen to the screams still frozen in my body. With you I speak my failure with you I hear my defeat with you I fight the battle to undo the words that hold me prisoner with you I find the words to love with you I find the words to hate.

Today my journey is long. The door I open is bursting with ghosts I cannot see beyond. With you my lover I find the courage to touch the ghosts to feel them dissolve under my skin. Behind the door we stand together. We see ourselves reflected in a room full of mirrors we watch our love as it grows and changes with every distortion of the mirrors as we step forward. Like the walls that surround us in this hall of mirrors our journey is not linear. Our bodies reflected in the mirrors we approach one another our bodies moulded by our gaze shaped by our journey.

* * *

Childhood

From my room I hear them speak they think I am a child I am already old much older than they are. In my mind I see maman I see her eyes wandering she is not listening to the conversation sometimes she nods she is not really there but they don't notice they lost their eyes as their faces outgrew their features. Papa laughs out loud he doesn't think it's funny he is tired I see sleep as it sits on his lap he pushes it away angry he likes to stay up late sometimes even if he is tired. I am big now they put me to bed they don't come to kiss me goodnight until the guests have gone then they remember I wait for their kiss. Until then I listen to them speak. Papa speaks of me he tells them secrets he has kept from me he says I'm wonderful she's great you know he says look what she's done yes says maman she reads already I can feel them smiling guests make them smile. I don't know why guests stay away the house is usually silent maman doesn't like it when I make noise my brother is little he is sleeping shhhh she says but she doesn't have to tell me I already know. You think I am little but really I am big much bigger than you are I am six I am two and a thousand.

In the morning I wake early I listen for the sound of papa's ring on the banister and then I know it is earlier than six. In the bedroom across the hall I hear maman pretending to be asleep. In the small room my brother screams he has diaper rash maman says I don't think so I think he just likes to wake the house after a dark night. I don't like him much he is not a girl so little with his dark black hair and he cries all of the time. Maman holds him in her arms I hear papa leave she feeds my brother with a bottle her eyes far away she thinks I am not looking they think I am a child I'm not I want to say but they don't listen no one listens to children.

I want to tell you about my childhood but there isn't much to tell I have been a child many times and in between I have been older than you will ever be. Today sitting in the café with all of the others sitting around me eating their eggs and toast bacon and home-fries I am among children many of them but they pretend they're big just like I pretended I was big when I was much smaller than the others.

Every year maman makes me a cake with raspberry jam between the chocolate layers with fudge on top and smarties. I blow out the candles and my aunt says what a big girl I am. If I could reach her face I would pinch her cheeks and smile then she would know that it hurts and maybe she wouldn't do it next year. When I grow up I'll never say you'll know better when you're grown up because as far as I can tell they don't know better and they're all quite big at least twice my size. Sometimes people still pinch my cheeks not often though because I am so big I can look over rooftops and step on grown-ups walking below.

* * *

From the window to my left I can see the world moving time at its heels. All around me I see sparkles of time held on invisible thread with fragments of childhoods left behind. In the leftovers on their plates the unfinished crusts the yellow of their yolks the fried potato they forgot to eat in all of these pieces there are glimpses of the childhoods they would rather deny. Talking about child-hood is not for them it is reserved for people like me who like to tell stories and for those who don't want to grow up. What they don't know is that they've betrayed them-selves with their messy plates they've revealed that their mature faces are nothing but masks to conceal the chil-dren they've covered up.

I can tell you a secret about being grown up but you must never repeat it aloud. The children we weren't in a world that grew up too fast those are the children we are today. You see, it's much safer to be a child when there aren't grown-ups around who are supposed to take care of you who are still children themselves having children. If maman were to make me a birthday cake today one like the ones she used to make it would have twice as many smarties and thicker fudge and most importantly it would have many more candles to blow out and I would wish many more wishes I would blow harder because my breath has strengthened and my wish would come true. When I was little my lungs were still too weak I never blew all of the candles at once I never got my wish.

Today I will tell you the story of my childhood it will be the story of my day we will pretend it is my birthday. Today I will blow out all of the candles on my cake and my wish will come true. My wish will be to tell the stories of all of those who sit and speak in hushed voices at the tables around me but we will pretend that this is my story because they will deny everything I say. That is another sign of adults concealing children. I will call this my story but you will know that this is also theirs and yours.

Twenty-five years ago I was born into this strange place people call the world but really I have lived a thousand years. Already on that day when I was dropped into space and time I knew I had lived many centuries but maman didn't like to store that many candles in the house so we kept up the pretense that my first day began at your side. From that moment I grew and grew sometimes my nose was unfortunate sometimes I had a bird's nest on my head but you really meant my hair your back is not long like mine you said meaning your waist is thick your face is long oval you said meaning the shape is not mine wide cheekbones your breasts are so large you said meaning a body is more beautiful without breasts to mar the line of the clothing you said standing in my clothes in front of the mirror. It should look like it does on the hanger like it does on me you didn't say. I want to be you maman I didn't say.

* * *

I am learning how to fly to get away from those words that seer me still to get away from the desire to cut off my breasts to hide in thick layers to keep your hands to keep my hands from my body. I have been learning to fly now for many years. I still crash sometimes in fact I did yesterday. If you look closely you'll see a bruise on my stomach but that only happens when I'm being too careful and I forget to let my wings move with the wind. I remember the first time I flew. It was the day papa announced to me that there was another child with maman in the hospital. He dressed me in the pink wool outfit the one with the bonnet that grandma made for me to go to the circus and we went to the hospital but when we got there they wouldn't let me in because they said I was too little. Papa let go of my hand and I let my feet float off the ground I flew high into the sky so high that soon I was looking through the window at papa and maman and the little one screaming at her side but they didn't know I was there because they think only angels can fly.

I didn't fly much after that. There was a time in my life when my feet became so heavy I could no longer leave the ground. I forgot to fly and then it was a long long time before I tried again and found I could lift myself high into the sky. I couldn't tell you even if I tried how long it was between those flights because time passes through me sometimes slowly sometimes quickly and I think that was one of those slow times.

These days I have to be a little more careful when I fly because I am big now and I have to watch to make sure my feet don't get stuck in chimneys and that I don't fly too close to satellite dishes because if I did the people watching TV would see me on their screens and who knows what might happen then.

* * *

The Convalescent

"Do not speak on, O convalescent!" thus his animals answered him; "but go out where the world awaits you like a garden. Go out to the roses and bees and dovecots. But especially to the songbirds, that you may learn from them how to sing! For singing is for the convalescent; the healthy can speak."

I am Zarathustra it is time for me to sing. I'm not sure you will understand my song perhaps it will not reach your ears but if you listen carefully you will hear the melody of my convalescence followed by the words of my health.

My day is a mountain range. In the early morning I open my eyes to the world I spread my wings and soar high the peaks barely touching my toes. Mid-morning arrives I sense the landing time approach. I slow down and feel my feet as they hold the earth firmly beneath them. As the sun begins to droop I feel my footing falter and I slide down the slippery slope falling into the abyss. By evening I have recovered from the crash and am ready once again to climb toward the peaks and fly.

It is mid-afternoon and I am waking up my head dizzy from the intensity of my fall. The descent steep today I feel the burden of the climb on my limbs. Far away I see the healthy ones still standing tall on the peak. I am a convalescent forever recovering from the fall. At night in my dreams I try to extend the bones the ligaments the muscles in my legs in order that someday I might be able to leap from peak to peak without falling into the abyss. High above me I see the sun a round yellow ball beckoning me. I know the bright sphere of light will call my name every time I fall as long as my will remains to conquer the mountain. Today the climb is long and awkward my body weak.

The hardest climbs deserve love stories. I have promised you a love story. Today I will sing to you while we climb side by side. If you listen to the symphony of sounds as they approach your body you will hear the most beautiful love story you have ever imagined. With every new note your feet will dance and before you have time to look up we will have reached the peak.

* * *

It is many chapters since I first laid my hands on your body. You are my lover yours is the body that sings to me in my dreams yours are the words from which my story is created. Once we sang together. I hadn't known you long my lover you asked me if I wanted to sing with you you pulled out your guitar together our voices separate and often out of tune we sang.

Today we sing together. It is late our bodies unaccustomed to one another the music creates a closeness we feel our bodies approach as the song holds us together. One by one we sing the songs you keep in a pile beside your guitar always the same ones the songs we are familiar with the music of the pasts we did not share. We are separate connected by songs we both sang before we knew each other. Through the songs we touch. We sing for hours the darkness dimming the first colours of the sun rising you ask if I want to follow you to your bed. I listen to the music as it fades into your question I know you are waiting for my answer I know I will follow you I am relieved that it is a question. Yes I smile. Together we climb the steps into the rising sun our bodies heavy with sleep. No longer protected by the songs of our past we stand facing one-another the bed closed before us. Our bodies still foreign to one-another we are silent as we slowly remove our clothing leaving a few layers of protection bits of our past still clinging to our skin. Soon we will soar together morning will come we will fly next to the sun but now the darkness has not yet risen out of its cave our feet still firmly implanted in the earth we face one-another our silence full of questions.

The songs still resonating in our bodies we lie on the cold white sheet. You cover me with a blanket your hand gently caressing my face. Like all lovers we are convalescents not yet recovered from the multitude of notes singing in our bodies as we approach one another as our bodies melt into love. We are alone in the sea that surrounds us. There is no experience that can guide us our touch the only navigator. Our eyes wide open we watch the sky the metamorphosis of light and colour exploding before us. Our bodies gently reaching touching caressing we prepare for our flight to the sun.

I don't remember when we first made love. In every glance we spoke our desire in every touch we felt our bodies soar into the light with every question we could not ask we touched a thousand answers. That night our bodies met in the closest intimacy I have ever known. That morning I landed on the sun.

Today we have been lovers for many nights we have flown together we have seen the sun sometimes bright orange sometimes magenta sometimes purple. Sometimes we have walked into the depths in the middle of the afternoon sometimes I have walked alone and you have reached down with your arm and pulled me out sometimes we have slept in the abyss. Today we have been lovers under many moons our bodies no longer foreign we have allowed night to descend around us we have given in and slept our exhaustion knowing we would soon fly again. Today I know your body intimately I know the crevasses I have felt the curves the hardness the softness I have felt your skin break open beneath my fingers I have felt you sigh I have felt the urgency in your breath. Today we no longer need the songs of our past.

* * *

In every Now, being begins; round every Here rolls the sphere There. The center is everywhere. Bent is the path of eternity.

Evening is approaching soon we will reach the peak the heights from which I will fall again the next time I lose my footing. My love story has distracted the pain from my ankles my body now strong with desire. Some of the larger bruises have already dispersed left behind in pockets of time along the way. Only the subtle marks remain as the signs of the fall on my body. As my feet lead me along the well-trodden path I am aware that within me lives the center that is the gateway to eternal return the center that is the secret of being. This morning before I fell I ignored the center. I covered the path to eternity with a thick dull cloth and I closed my eyes in order not to see the Now from which my center begins. Sometimes I forget.

The day is long. Often I search for the first sign of darkness. I look forward to concealing myself behind the sun's shadow. From this position I dream and watch the world without fear of being uncovered. The one I run from cannot find me in the shadows of the darkness. You look for me in the reflection of the daylight or in the spotlight of my nightmares. You cannot see when my eyes light up the dimming night. You are the bearer of memory the culprit of my pain the one I long to throw up the one who pushes me over the edge of the precipice. This afternoon you almost caught up to me as my arm was reaching for the last branch as my feet approached the peak you stood before me your face grimacing you laughed so hard you scared away the trees and left me dangling in mid-air. But underneath me I felt the wind she held me up and pushed me over the top she waited by my side until you grunted and walked the other way. You are not patient the detector of my weakness but your resistance is strong. Without the wind at my side you may have had the strength to overpower me. Today I may have had to sleep in the abyss. It did not happen the wind reminds me that there is a There in every Here she says there is a bend in the path below my feet that will confuse you and steer you in the wrong direction. As long as I follow the crooked path you will not find my center. You always looks for straight lines.

I am the convalescent. I wake to the sounds of the world resounding in my ears I look for health among the lines and wrinkles of my body. In my convalescence I see a direction it is not clear the path is strewn with leaves and mud and wild flowers I must walk step by step uncovering my way a little at a time. Impatience leads me to the other path that points straight ahead toward self-destruction. I have followed that path before. It is not the path of health nor the path of convalescence. It is your path. You own shares in the nightmares that cross it. It is the path of resentment. It is the path that leads nowhere. Bent is the path of eternity says Zarathustra bent is the path of love I say. The language of desire leads to the center from which the Here the There the Now and the Then begin. The language of Desire is my link to health it is the hand that connects me to you my love.

* * *

The Body

I cannot write the end of my body. You cannot read this chapter and see it as the last. There is no end to my body. In my toenail I see my reflection. I am a circle. There is no end to the story written on my body.

I was going to write you a love-story, a story about love. I was going to trace the lines on my body. I was going to explore the wrinkles and find the holes and the gaps in my story. I promised you a love story. I promised you a happy ending.

The chapters I am not going to write are the missing chapters. They are the mystery chapters. They are the chapters that offer a conclusion. They are your conclusion. They are for you to write.

* * *

Finding the perfect mango is a very elusive endeavour. Even I the seasoned mango eater cannot tell you how to choose a mango and be sure that it is the mango you have been longing for. Mangoes are a very tricky fruit and very deceptive. Sometimes my hand grabs for the most beautiful one the one with the bright red and yellow skin the one that feels soft to my touch but then when I bite into it the juice is rancid and I have been fooled by vanity. The opposite is not true either. I have chosen the ugliest mangoes only to find that they taste as bad as they look. And yet mangoes are unquestionably the fruit of desire. There is nothing like a perfect mango.

If you do find a perfect mango I can tell you that eating it will be the experience you always hoped it would be. If you are like me and you like the skin the first thing you must do is discard the bitter stem. Then bite carefully down onto the skin and pull with your teeth. If it is the perfect mango that you have found you will find that the skin peels back in pieces just the right size. Eat the skin slowly. When all you have left is the fruit perfectly peeled yellow orange dripping a little in your hands take your first mouthful. Don't worry if the sweet juice drips onto your fingers and most importantly don't use a cloth to wipe it off. Your hands are now part of the mango. Lick them as you would the delicious mango. Your body is the perfect mango.

Every day I crave mangoes. I look forward to the stickiness. I look forward to the challenge of eating mangoes without covering my shirt with yellow stains. I look forward to the yellow stains. Today I ate two mangoes. I am sad because I am finishing my book. I thought writing a mango into my story might give my book the delicious ending that it lacks. I don't like endings.

* * *

This is a love story. It does not have a happy ending. It does not have an ending. August is here and the air is cooler. When I began writing my love-story the air was still. Today I can feel a breeze.

My hands still sticky from the mango I trace the outline of my story onto my body. On the surface nothing has changed. I do not need a mirror to see the reflection of my body. I probe deeper with my fingers. One by one I uncover the changes. My story has left marks on my body. On my right thigh I find the discarded sentence from page eighteen. On my baby toe I feel the leftover commas. On my eye I see the pages I could not write. I follow the trajectory of my body. I am searching for something I have not yet found. I want to give it to you. My fingers are tired of searching. I cannot give you the missing chapters. I cannot give you the ending. I cannot give you my body.

It is mid-afternoon it is mid-chapter it is the middle of my life I feel the pain in my stomach the pain of the middle. The middle scares me it is much more difficult than beginnings or endings yet here I am in the middle of my day in the middle of my story with you waiting at my side. I feel your eyes on me I feel your questions and I know there are no answers. I have let you touch my body I have let you see me I have let you feel the memories as they appeared on the page. Fractured and ravaged I have lent you my body. Today I feel my body swimming into a new skin. I am shedding the old, the old engraved on the new.

This is a love story, a story about love. It is the story of my body as it appears to me in the morning. It is the story of my body as my fingers hit the keys and the words appear on the page. It is the pain I feel when I wash away the vomit from the bathroom floor. It is the ecstasy I feel when my lover's hands carve desire onto my body. It is the joy of knowing that there is no ending.

Afterward

Julietta Singh

I was several years into a PhD in literature before I realized that I had mistaken the term *afterword* for its homophone, *afterward*. This slip is understandable, not only through the logics of sound but also through the conceptual registers that each term evokes. One signals the words that come after other words, written by another writer as a response to a primary text. And the other, my mistake, summons an orientation that comes after those words – one that seems both discrete from and adjacent to the primary text. Both *afterword* and *afterward* signal a movement from something before into something after, and from one body into another. But these seemingly discrete bodies – the words and the words that come after – are bodies that touch, bodies that make and unmake each other.

I first read *The Perfect Mango* shortly after having spent three unexpectedly intense and enchanted days with Erin Manning. My friend and collaborator, Nathan Snaza, had invited Erin to give a workshop at the University of Richmond. We knew Erin's work as a philosopher and artist, had studied her writing, but neither of us were prepared for the *feeling* that Erin's presence would produce. At once ethereal and profoundly substantive, Erin's spirit was captivating. An instantaneous mix of intimacy, energy, and hope flooded through us, unequivocally binding us together. It is a feeling that is still and will always be in circulation; when I feel lost, I open myself and let it in.

It was during that visit that Erin first mentioned *The Perfect Mango,* a text she had written nearly a quarter of a century ago that had gone out of print and been quite forgotten in the trajectory of her prolific career. A text she had composed in a concentrated time, over nineteen days, in a state of absolute desperation. A text she wrote because she had to, because her survival depended on it. Through the long breathless sentences, the recurring expressions of desire to write herself into being – not to be read but *to be learned by heart* – I came to understand Erin as a being that lives in a different time. That young woman who narrates herself into life, who is twenty-five or a thousand, is scrambling to situate herself in and against time, to make sense of a chrono-logic that cannot account for her.

The Perfect Mango is a book about the body, about learning to see it as an entity that has *no end,* something that is never permanently marked by the violence of history, that can *swim into a new skin.* The sexual trauma that haunts this book is being painted and purged across its pages, and the young woman who refuses to remain caught in the capture of trauma is also learning to feed herself, to become a body-being that will endure in new forms and through new forms of mutual making. I know this girl, for she is many. I love this girl, as I love us all – we misfits whose hurt provokes us to live through other styles and modes of becoming-together.

Afterward, after wading through *the maze of paint and vomit* that constitutes this beautiful book, we surface broken and in love. Broken and in love, no longer having to hold ourselves up to a narrative of completion, but letting ourselves suspend together, in various forms of contact, in life. And there is no mistake in this, in the afterward that *The Perfect Mango* summons and lives out.

Printed in Great Britain
by Amazon